ON THE ROAD WITH U2
my musical journey

By Deena Dietrich

Dedication

This book is dedicated to my parents, who are my best friends, for all their love and support and without whom I would not have the confidence or the freedom to pursue my passions.

Thanks to all the U2 fans in the world especially Cindy, Mike, Tasha, Jenny, Abbey, Paola, Matt and Melissa who have been crucial to my musical journey. A special thank you to Kari Moore who took the photograph for the cover of this book.

Last but not least, a huge THANK YOU to Larry, Bono, Edge and Adam without whom none of this would be possible and my life would be very different, I would be very different.

Contents

Introduction 4

Before the Musical Journey 6

Zoo TV 11

PopMart 24

Elevation 35

Vertigo 80

360 (2009) 93

360 (2011) 116

Introduction

It is finally here, the last day of my musical journey. My last U2 360 show, my 75th U2 show overall and my last chance to meet Larry. Hard to believe I left my house 74 days ago on this quest to see every U2 360 concert in the United States, and as it turned out also a quest to meet Larry Mullen. I wore the same "Larry Mullen Band" shirt and straw cowboy hat to every show, and I have talked with Bono twice about meeting Larry. Will today, July 26, 2011 in Pittsburgh, be the day Larry comes out to greet the fans, to meet me?

I began that day in Pittsburgh just as I had the past two and a half months for the previous 15 U2 360 shows. I walked my dogs (Elvis and Cilla), ate breakfast, watched television, napped, ordered a pizza for after the concert and then went to the stadium around 2pm to wait for U2 to arrive. I met my friends Abbey and Anisha in the lobby of my hotel, and we took the free shuttle over to Heinz Field even though it was close enough to walk. It was a beautiful day, quite pleasant for the end of July with temperatures in the mid-80s, sunny, breezy, and not humid. I saw many friends old and new, but the surprise was Matt, Melissa, Melissa's parents and Kim. I had no idea they were coming all the way from the West Coast. I was very happy to see them, and it turned out to be very fortunate for me as well.

U2 arrived just around 5pm. Bono and Edge came out to greet the fans. I could not get close enough to talk with them, but I did see Larry and Adam get out of their cars and walk inside. Matt and Melissa talked with Bono and selflessly told him about me and how I had driven to every U.S. show and would like to meet Larry. Brian, Bono's security guy, told them to wait there and he would see what he could do. Brian came out later and told me Larry was in a meeting, but he told Larry about me and said that Bono told Larry about me. I couldn't believe this! Bono was talking to Larry about ME! Brian took my phone number and said he would look for me inside. He also gave us wristbands for the soundboard and for the red zone.

      Even though I had the credentials to stand wherever I wanted, I went to my usual spot on Edge's side of the inner circle to wait for U2 to enter. I kept checking my phone anxiously waiting for Larry to call me. Abbey was with me, as was Deb and her husband and Melissa's parents. Brian came over and told me he was still working on getting me to meet Larry. I had no idea how this was going to happen. Maybe I would finally get to go back stage! The opening band, Interpol, took the stage around 7:45 and played their usual 45-minute set. About a half hour later, the lights went down, "Space Oddity" began, and U2 made their way out of the tunnel on Adam's side where Melissa and Matt were standing. My heart sank because I knew my last chance to meet Larry was over as this was my last U2 show. But then I noticed Larry was not the first one walking out as usual. Adam and Edge were first with Larry and Bono behind them. Then somehow Larry moved in front of them. As Larry walked up the ramp, he locked eyes with me and was smiling. What was about to happen next I could never have imagined 24 years prior when I first discovered U2…

Before the Musical Journey

My very first U2 poster, circa 1987
(I labeled it with their names, so I could remember who was who.)

The Joshua Tree

It was March 1987. I was a freshman in high school. Being an only child with no older brothers or sisters to introduce me to cool music, my musical taste at 14 was Top 40. My favorites were Wham and Madonna. I also loved Tears for Fears, Huey Lewis and Cyndi Lauper - typical 80s pop. But one day in class that all changed.

A classmate of mine was flipping through one of those teen music magazines and stopped at a picture of U2. She said they were the ones who sang that new song "With or Without You." I had heard it and liked it. I sort of remembered their song "Pride" that was out a few years before. I noticed one of the four guys, the drummer, in the picture was very good looking. To a 14 year-old, it is very important for a band you like to have a cute boy to crush on. Since Wham had broken up, I needed another band to obsess over. Soon my locker would be decorated with pictures of Larry Mullen Jr. It wasn't just Larry's looks that drove me to him. As I would learn later, it was his personality. I find Larry's no nonsense, tell it like it is, I don't care what anyone else thinks personality very appealing. Plus, he founded U2, a.k.a The Larry Mullen Band.

I immediately bought the tapes of *The Joshua Tree* and *Under a Blood Red Sky*. For the next several months, those two tapes were all I listened to. That summer I walked along the beach in Ocean City, Maryland carrying my boom box blaring "I Still Haven't Found What I'm Looking For," which is still my favorite song today. "With or Without You" introduced me to U2, but "I Still Haven't Found What I'm Looking For" made me a U2 fan. It is more than just my favorite song. "I Still Haven't Found What I'm Looking For" gives me a feeling of sheer joy and comfort and touches my soul like no other song. I love a lot of U2 songs, most U2 songs, but "I Still Haven't

Found What I'm Looking For" is on a completely different level. "I Still Haven't Found What I'm Looking For" has literally been my theme song. It says that life is about the journey, not the destination. I am enjoying my journey, the quest for what truly makes me happy.

Besides "I Still Haven't Found What I'm Looking For," my favorites off *The Joshua Tree* are "Red Hill Mining Town" (I was obsessed with this song!), "Running to Stand Still," "Trip Through Your Wires," "In God's Country," and b-sides "Luminous Times" (my second all-time favorite song), "Walk to the Water," "Deep in the Heart" and "Spanish Eyes." I love the b-sides of *The Joshua Tree* as much as, if not more than, the songs that actually made it onto the album.

Along with *The Joshua Tree*, I bought *Under a Blood Red Sky* that day in 1987. Four years prior, U2 had released their first live album on November 21, 1983. The fans have nicknamed the album "Red Rocks" because it was recorded at Red Rocks Park and Amphitheater outside of Denver, Colorado – home of my beloved Denver Broncos. This performance was also made into a concert movie. The *Under a Blood Red Sky* concert film was my first U2 "concert" experience. It was the first time I saw U2 perform "live." I watched that concert over and over again. My favorites off *Under a Blood Red Sky* are "October" into "New Year's Day," "Sunday Bloody Sunday," "Gloria" and "Party Girl." Red Rocks is when I first heard and fell in love with "New Year's Day," and it is still one of my favorites today. And to this day, I still hear Bono saying, "This song is not a rebel song. This song is 'Sunday Bloody Sunday'" every time "Sunday Bloody Sunday" is played. The *Under a Blood Red Sky* live album and concert video is so ingrained in my head.

By the time *Rattle and Hum* came out in 1988, I had all of U2's albums and recorded all of their performances on television. My favorites of the other four albums, besides *The*

Joshua Tree and *Under a Blood Red Sky*, were and are *October* and *The Unforgettable Fire*. *October* is a very underrated U2 album, but I love it. It is a very drum-driven album. And as we all know, it's all about drums. October is my favorite month. I was born in October. My favorite season of Fall is in October. To me, October symbolizes the changing of the seasons and the beginning of my favorite time of year. One of the themes of U2's album *October* is change. My favorite songs off *October* are "Rejoice," "October" and "Gloria."

The Unforgettable Fire is another standout for me from those early years. I thought it was a great bridge between my first U2 albums *Under a Blood Red Sky* (which had songs from the first three albums) and *The Joshua Tree*. Tracks "Pride," "Bad" and "Unforgettable Fire" have always been favorites of mine. "Bad" is amazing live and "Unforgettable Fire" has always held a special place in my heart mostly because of the video. I love Larry in the "Unforgettable Fire" video, in fact the *UF* era is my favorite look for Larry. I love when Larry looks up and flashes that sweet smile.

On November 4, 1988, exactly one month after my 16th birthday, I piled a bunch of my friends into my GMC Jimmy and drove to the movie theater to see the premiere of U2's *Rattle and Hum*. I don't remember buying the tape, but I do remember going to the movie theater to see *Rattle and Hum*. It was like going to my first U2 concert. I was only 14, almost 15, when the Joshua Tree tour came to town, but my mom said I was too young to go. So for me, seeing *Rattle and Hum* was like being at a U2 concert, and you always remember your first. People were dancing in the aisles. As if seeing U2 perform in concert wasn't exciting enough, *Rattle and Hum* also showed U2 recording in Sun Studio and touring my beloved Elvis Presley's Graceland in Memphis. Being a huge Elvis fan as well, my worlds were colliding!

I loved *Rattle and Hum* almost as much as *The Joshua Tree*. To me it was just an extension of it, sort of a *Joshua Tree* part two. My favorites songs off *Rattle and Hum* were and still are "Heartland," "Love Rescue Me," "Angel of Harlem," and b-sides "Hallelujah Here She Comes" and "A Room at the Heartbreak Hotel." To this day, my favorite versions of "I Still Haven't Found What I'm Looking For," "Bad" and "Pride" are from *Rattle and Hum*. Those versions play in my head every time I listen to those songs, the *Rattle and Hum* versions are what I think of every time. I don't think I can truly express how special *Rattle and Hum* is to me, and how crucial it was in growing my love for U2.

Even though I had all of U2's albums, *The Joshua Tree* was what I listened to constantly from 1987 to 1991, along with *Rattle and Hum. The Joshua Tree* was also all I watched for five years. I taped everything off MTV, the documentaries, the videos, the concerts, the award show appearances and the interviews. My favorite is the first U2 I ever taped off television, the documentary *Outside It's America.* I know it by heart because I used to watch it every day. Even though it has been 28 years, *The Joshua Tree* is still my favorite album. It is truly a part of me. I think because it was my first U2 album and all I listened to and watched for five years. It is just so ingrained in me. Its songs are second nature to me. Like being home, they are comforting. *The Joshua Tree* changed my life.

Zoo TV

Bono and Me Giants Stadium August 1992
(Photo by Mike Elms)

Acthung Y'all!

After four and a half years of devouring every U2 song, video, interview and appearance, there was finally new music. *Achtung Baby* was released on November 19, 1991. This was the first time I was a U2 fan for a new release. A new album meant a new tour, and I would finally get to see U2 in concert. With all this excitement and anticipation, I put *Achtung Baby* on and hated it. It was just SO different from anything U2 had ever done, SO different from what I had been constantly listening to the past four years. I listened to *Achtung Baby* over and over and over again. By about the tenth listen, I fell in love with *Achtung Baby,* and it is now my second favorite U2 album. (I say second, even though it's technically third behind *The Joshua Tree* and *Rattle and Hum*, because I always lump them together.)

What turned me around were the lyrics. When I got past the oh so different music of *Achtung Baby*, and it was really different, I realized the lyrics were just as powerful, if not more so, than the previous U2 albums I had loved so much. And for me it's all about the lyrics, and the drums. "Who's Gonna Ride Your Wild Horses" is my favorite song off *Achtung Baby* and one of my top five favorite U2 songs ever. It is a very emotional and angry song. In fact, I made my college boyfriend sit down and listen to the lyrics as I read them to him after he had broken up with me. If I could have written a song about us, "Who's Gonna Ride Your Wild Horses" would have been it. Other favorites of mine off *Achtung Baby* are "One," "So Cruel," "Acrobat," and "Tryin to Throw Your Arms Around the World," but really all the songs are my favorites. I can't pick a bad one. There is not one that I skip, now. I didn't really appreciate the hits "Mysterious Ways," "The Fly" or "Even Better Than the Real Thing" until much later.

Achtung Baby was the start of "it's all about drums," one of my favorite quotes that I have repeated constantly over the past 20 years. The first time I ever heard it was on the *Achtung Baby* documentary when Larry said, "I don't think the lyrics are worth a shit to be honest if you ask me, I think it's all about drums." I love the album cover for *Achtung Baby*. For years, I was looking for those U2 rings, and finally found them. I love the collage of pictures as the album cover. It reminds me of the ZooTv tour and everything about that era.

Achtung Baby means so much to me because it was the music of my first U2 tour, Zoo Tv. I was a sophomore in college, so I was finally allowed go to concerts! I had a subscription to *Propaganda*, U2's fan magazine, which gave me an opportunity to buy tickets to one or two concerts before they went on sale. I went to two shows on the first leg of the Zoo Tv tour and six shows on the Outside Broadcast leg. This was the start of my musical journey on the road with U2. I was almost 20 and drove up and down the East Coast going to U2 concerts making great friends and visiting great sights along the way.

The months between the release of *Achtung Baby* and the start of the Zoo TV tour were spent constantly watching and listening to U2. My U2 buddy Mike and I would spend hours and hours just watching U2 footage over and over that we had taped on VHS: MTV specials, interviews, videos, etc. It was during this time I transformed from U2 fan to U2 fanatic.

My 1st U2 Show – March 7, 1992 – Hampton

My musical journey on the road with U2 began in Hampton, Virginia on March 7, 1992 when I was 19. This fifth show of the Zoo TV tour was the first one that was within driving distance from me. On the day of the concert, my best friend, Cindy, and I drove four hours from Ellicott City, Maryland to Hampton, Virginia. Back in those days, there was no need to get to the city of a concert a day early because there was no general admission. We had actual assigned seats on the floor.

We checked into our hotel and immediately walked across the street to the Hampton Coliseum, even though it was hours before the concert was to begin. We saw a small circle of people with a big microphone hovering over them. As we got closer, we realized Bono was in the middle of that circle of fans and reporters! I didn't speak with him, but got close enough to hear what Bono was saying to everyone else. For my first U2 show, I sat in the fourth row in front of Edge. Bruce Hornsby and Phil Joanou walked in from behind the stage and passed by us on their way to the VIP section at the soundboard. The Pixies opened, and I did not like them at all. But then again, I just wanted to hear U2. I had been waiting five long years since the release of *The Joshua Tree* to see U2 in concert!

The set list for my very first U2 show, Zoo TV March 7, 1992, in Hampton, VA was as follows: Zoo Station, Even Better Than The Real Thing, Mysterious Ways, The Fly, One, Until The End Of The World, Who's Gonna Ride Your Wild Horses, Trying to Throw Your Arms Around the World, Angel Of Harlem, Satellite Of Love, Bad-All I Want Is You-Bullet The Blue Sky, Running to Stand Still, Where the Streets , Pride, I Still Haven't Found, Desire, Ultraviolet (Light My Way), With or Without You. According to U2gigs.com, this was the only time on the ZooTV Tour "'The Fly' is played after "Even Better Than the Real Thing" and "Mysterious Ways," rather than before."

U2 show #2 – March 10, 1992 – Philadelphia

Three days later my U2 friend Mike and I drove two hours up to Philadelphia, Pennsylvania for my second U2 show on March 10, 1992. This was the closest show to me on the first leg of the Zoo TV tour. U2 did not play Baltimore or Washington, DC, so Philadelphia was the next closest city. When we arrived at the Spectrum, we saw Bono in the parking lot talking with fans. For this show, I was ninth row. The Pixies opened again, but this time I hid in the bathroom during their set.

The set list only varied a little from the Hampton show. The set list for the Zoo TV show in Philadelphia on March 10, 1992 was as follows: Zoo Station, The Fly, Even Better Than The Real Thing, Mysterious Ways, One, Until The End Of The World, Who's Gonna Ride Your Wild Horses, Trying to Throw Your Arms..., Angel Of Harlem, Satellite Of Love, Bad-All I Want Is You-Bullet The Blue Sky, Running to Stand Still, Where the Streets , Pride, I Still Haven't Found, Desire, Ultraviolet (Light My Way), With or Without You, Love Is Blindness.

U2 show #3 – August 7, 1992 – Hershey

In the summer of 1992, U2 ditched the arenas for stadiums for their Zoo TV Outside Broadcast Tour. It was on this leg of the tour that my musical journey on the road with U2 truly started. I began to meet U2 fans and toured around with them. My U2 friend Mike and I traveled to all these Zoo TV shows together and would meet the same fans at various shows.

Mike and I found out U2 was going to be rehearsing for a week in Hershey, Pennsylvania for their Zoo TV Outside Broadcast Tour. U2 wanted to rehearse at Memorial Stadium in Baltimore, but the community freaked out and protested declaring U2 would bring drugs and loud rock and roll music into their neighborhood at all hours of the night. Never mind what it would have done for Baltimore's economy to have U2 and their crew in the city for a week. So instead of driving 20 minutes to Baltimore, Mike and I drove two hours up to Hershey a couple of nights and sat outside the stadium to listen to U2 rehearse. We never actually saw the band, but we did hear U2 play for the first and last time "Acrobat" and "So Cruel" sitting on the curb outside Hershey Stadium.

We got tickets to the Zoo TV Outside Broadcast Rehearsal Concert on August 7, 1992 at Hershey Park Stadium. Tickets were only $15 and the proceeds went to local charities. We were way in the back, but at least we were there and it was a great show! Instead of starting off the show with "Zoo Station" like all the other Zoo Tv shows, U2 began with "Sunday Bloody Sunday," "New Year's Day" and "Pride" before going into their regular set starting with "Zoo Station." "Pride" was played a second time before the encore. This was the first time I had ever heard "New Year's Day" and "Sunday Bloody Sunday," since they did not play them on the first leg of the Zoo Tv tour. Edge sang "Van Dieman's Land," the first and only time I have ever heard it live. This U2 show was on the day before Edge's birthday, so Bono led the audience in singing "Happy Birthday" to the Edge.

The set list for the Zoo TV Outside Broadcast Rehearsal Concert in Hershey on August 7, 1992 was as follows: Sunday Bloody Sunday, New Year's Day, Pride, Zoo Station, The Fly, Even Better Than The Real Thing, Mysterious Ways, One-Unchained Melody, Until The End Of The World, Who's Gonna Ride Your Wild Horses, Van

Diemen's Land, Trying to Throw Your Arms Around the World, Angel of Harlem, When Love Comes To Town, All I Want Is You, Bullet The Blue Sky, Running to Stand Still, Where the Streets , Pride, Desire, Ultraviolet (Light My Way), With or Without You, Love Is Blindness.

U2 show #4 – August 12, 1992 – East Rutherford

Four days later on August 11, 1992, Mike, Jonathan, Kelly and I drove up to East Rutherford, New Jersey for the official opening of the ZooTV Outside Broadcast tour at Giants Stadium. Three guys and myself staying in one hotel room in New Jersey for three nights. I guess my mom was over that whole I'm too young to go to concerts thing. I was almost 20 after all.

Even though Opening Night had been pushed back a day to August 12th, Mike and I still went over to the stadium on the 11th. We snuck into the stadium and somehow got up onto the stage and touched the trabants, which were used to light the stage. (Trabants were little throw away cars the Germans used to escape East Germany in to West Germany.) Mike and I eventually got kicked out of the stadium, but we didn't get into trouble. That night we tried to figure out where U2 was staying, but we failed and ended up waiting outside on the hotel curb huddled near a bus keeping warm from the fumes. I don't remember why it was so cold in August, but it was.

The next day all four of us went over to Giants Stadium early. There were a bunch of fans standing outside on the afternoon of August 12th waiting for U2 to arrive. Bono walked out in his all black, all velvet suit. I could not believe how short he was. In my excitement and the fact I have no filter, I think I exclaimed, "Look how little he is!" But he was far enough away not to hear me, I hope. Bono walked down the line of fans, talking with each of us one at a time, and taking his time to sign autographs and take pictures. It was a very organized, single file, calm line with no barricades and only a couple security guys, nothing like the craziness it is today.

When Bono came to me, he noticed the shirt I had made with "One" on it, which looked very similar to the "One" on the video. I handed Bono my *Outside It's America* book for him to autograph. I noticed he was taking a while, so I looked at what he was doing and saw he was misspelling my name. I said, "No, Deena is spelled with two e's." He kind of gave me this sly smile as if to say 'are you correcting me? I'm bono?' In my book, Bono wrote, "A nice t-shirt Din…Deena Bono 92" As soon as he was finished, I threw my camera to Mike, so he could take a picture of me and Bono, both with our big sunglasses. Almost knocking me down, Bono hugged me putting his arms around my waist and resting his head on my shoulder. After the photo, I asked Bono if U2 would ever play "Heartland" in concert because it was one of my favorites. He said, "Yeah that's a great song. We're thinking of putting out an album of b-sides soon." Huh? That's not what I asked. That was my first encounter with Bono, and what a great encounter it was.

Bono then went to my friend Jonathan, the only one of us who wasn't really a U2 fan. Bono drew boobs on Jonathan's shirt writing "Bono got on my tits" and autographed it. Jonathan was embarrassed to walk around the rest of the day with boobs on his shirt and kept complaining Bono ruined his shirt. I am sure most fans would not mind at all if Bono "ruined" their shirt. After Bono talked with everyone and walked back inside, Larry drove by us on his motorcycle and waved. Unfortunately he did not stop, but I did get a picture, then I ran away screaming. Larry just has that affect on me. It would be another nine years before I would actually meet Larry Mullen Jr.

Our seats for opening night were in the second section back on the floor in the fifth row. Larry sang "Dirty Old Town" as only he can, a sort of screaming and growling. I was so excited that Jonathan tried to hold me back, so I hit him causing him to fall off his chair. Lou Reed joined U2 on the B Stage for "Satellite of Love," and this performance was used for the rest of the tour via video.

The set list for Opening Night of the Zoo TV Outside Broadcast Tour on August 12, 1992 at Giants Stadium was as follows: Zoo Station, The Fly, Even Better Than The Real Thing, Mysterious Ways, One-Unchained Melody, Until The End Of The World, Who's Gonna Ride Your Wild Horses, Dirty Old Town, Trying to Throw Your Arms Your Arms Around the World, Angel of Harlem, When Love Comes to Town, Satellite Of Love, Bad-All I Want Is You, Bullet The Blue Sky, Running to Stand Still, Where the Streets , Pride, I Still Haven't Found-Stand By Me, Desire, Ultraviolet (Light My Way), With or Without You, Love Is Blindness.

U2 show #5 – August 13, 1992 – East Rutherford

The next night August 13th, our seats were closer. We were in the front section on the floor in the eighth row on the left (Edge's side). When Bono was leaving the main stage to walk down the catwalk to the B Stage, I pushed my way through to the walkway. The security guy stopped me. I pointed behind him and yelled, "Look he's right behind you!" He let me pass and I stood at the catwalk as Bono walked by. During "Desire," I caught a Zoo Dollar as they flew through the air.

The set list for the second Zoo TV show at Giants Stadium on August 13, 1992 was as follows: Zoo Station, The Fly, Even Better Than The Real Thing, Mysterious Ways, One-She's a Mystery to Me, Until The End Of The World, New Year's Day, Trying to Throw Your Arms Around the World, Angel Of Harlem, When Love Comes To Town, I Still Haven't Found , All I Want Is You, Sunday Bloody Sunday, Bullet The Blue Sky, Running to Stand Still, Where the Streets , Pride, Desire, With or Without You, Love Is Blindness.

U2 show #6 – August 15, 1992 – DC

Two days later, Mike and I were back in our hometown for two more Zoo TV shows. Well, sort of our hometown. As close at the Zoo Tv tour was going to get to Ellicott City, Maryland. We were at RFK Stadium in Washington, DC in the rain. I met Bono again, and he autographed the picture of the two of us from Giants Stadium. I showed him the picture and said, "We look great, don't we?" Bono was not as talkative as he was in Jersey. I think the rain made him grumpy.

U2 ended both shows in DC on August 15 and 16, 1992 with Elvis' "Can't Help Falling In Love" in honor of the 15th anniversary of the death of Elvis Presley on August 16, 1977. For the first show, I was in the front center floor section in the third row. Bono knelt in front of us and sang "Can't Help Falling in Love." As an avid Elvis fan, this was an amazing, unforgettable moment for me! For the rest of the tour, U2 ended the show with "Can't Help Falling in Love."

The set list for the first Zoo TV show in DC August 15, 1992 in DC was as follows: Zoo Station, The Fly, Even Better Than The Real Thing, Mysterious Ways, One-She's a Mystery to Me, Until The End Of The World, New Year's Day, Trying to

Throw Your Arms Around the World, Angel Of Harlem-Dancing Queen, When Love Comes to Town, I Still Haven't Found-Stand By Me, All I Want Is You, Sunday Bloody Sunday, Bullet The Blue Sky, Running to Stand Still, Where the Streets , Pride, Desire, With or Without You, Love Is Blindness, Can't Help Falling in Love.

U2 show #7 – August 16, 1992 – DC

The next night for the second Zoo TV show in DC, I sat in the eighth row of the front floor section on the right (Adam's side). The set list for August 16, 1992 was as follows: Zoo Station, The Fly, Even Better Than The Real Thing, Mysterious Ways, One-Unchained Melody, Until The End Of The World, New Year's Day, Trying to Throw Your Arms Your Arms Around the World, Angel Of Harlem, I Still Haven't Found, Satellite of Love, Bad, Sunday Bloody Sunday, Bullet The Blue Sky, Running to Stand Still, Where the Streets Have No Name, Pride, Desire, Ultraviolet (Light My Way), With or Without You, Love Is Blindness, Can't Help Falling in Love.

U2 show #8 – September 3, 1992 – Philadelphia

My final Zoo TV show was a few weeks later on September 3, 1992 at Veterans Stadium in Philadelphia, Pennsylvania. There were two shows and I was supposed to go to both shows, but was moving back to College Park so I only went to the second show. It was raining in Philadelphia, so security let the few of us waiting outside the stadium inside for the sound check. We were also excited because our friend Maggie, who wrote a fanzine, got us Hospitality passes, but all that got us were some sodas and chips. We didn't see U2 back stage at all, but we did get to hear "Whiskey in a Jar" and "When Loves Comes to Town."

The set list for my final Zoo TV show in Philly on September 3, 1992 was as follows: Zoo Station, The Fly, Even Better Than The Real Thing, Mysterious Ways, One-Unchained Melody, Until The End Of The World, New Year's Day, Whiskey In The Jar, Trying to Throw Your Arms Your Arms Around the World, Angel Of Harlem, When Love Comes to Town, I Still Haven't Found , Satellite of Love, Bad-All I Want Is You, Bullet The Blue Sky, Running to Stand Still, Where the Streets Have No Name, Pride, Desire, With or Without You, Love Is Blindness, Can't Help Falling in Love.

Post Zoo TV Thoughts

My first U2 tour was over. Primus and Disposable Heroes of Hiphoprosy opened all the shows I saw on the Zoo TV Outside Broadcast tour, except for the rehearsal concert in Hershey. Primus had a popular song called "Jerry Was a Racecar Driver" and U2 had been using Disposable's "Television Drug of a Nation" to open the shows. This went along well with their television-themed tour, complete with big screen tvs and Bono's channel flipping.

A few things that stand out in my memory, other than meeting Bono, are Adam introducing "Trying to Throw Your Arms Around the World" with the grocery cart, the belly dancer for "Mysterious Ways," Larry twirling the Trabant car light on the B Stage before "Satellite of Love," Bono's grand entrance during "Zoo Station," but mostly the "Hallelujah" chorus at the end of "Running to Stand Still" – it gave me chills every time I heard it, and still does today. The Zoo TV tour will always hold a special place in my heart as it was my first U2 tour.

Zooropa

U2 released *Zooropa* the summer following the Zoo TV tour. It was the first time I ever bought a cd, as opposed to a record or tape. Mike and I drove about 45 minutes to Tower Records in Rockville, Maryland at midnight July 5, 1993 to buy *Zooropa*. It had a similar sound to *Achtung Baby*, but I didn't like it as much. My favorites off *Zooropa* are "Dirty Day," "The First Time" and "Zooropa." U2 did not tour America in support of *Zooropa*. I would have to wait four more years for a new album and another tour.

PopMart

PopMart Columbus, OH 1997
(Photo by Deena Dietrich)

Pop Music

Five years later, U2 released *Pop* March 3, 1997. Unlike when I first listened to *Achtung Baby*, I didn't dislike *Pop* at first listen, but I didn't love it either. It only took a few listens to fall in love with *Pop*. It wasn't as big of a departure from *Achtung Baby* to *Pop* as it was from *The Joshua Tree* to *Achtung Baby*. I loved the first single "Discotheque" mainly because of the video. It was basically U2 dressed as the Village People doing pelvic thrusts, which I found hysterical. A lot of people didn't get the humor though.

People criticized *Pop* for being too techno and not enough of like the old U2, but why would a band want to keep creating the same songs over and over. If you get past the "techno" sound of Pop, which by the way I enjoy, and just listen to the lyrics they are as strong as anything U2 had ever done. In fact, one of my favorite U2 songs of all time, "Gone," is from *Pop*. Another amazing song from Pop is "Please," which would become very poignant a few years later. Other favorites of mine are "Staring at the Sun," "If You Wear That Velvet Dress" and the aforementioned "Discotheque."

U2 announced their PopMart Tour at a Kmart in New York City. I ran home from college to watch the press conference on MTV. Just a month after *Pop* was released, U2 went on the road for their PopMart Tour. I graduated college (after a long seven-year on-and-off-again process) and within a few days I was on the road with U2 on the PopMart Tour.

U2 show #9 – May 22, 1997 – Pittsburgh

My first PopMart show was on May 22, 1997 at Three Rivers Stadium in Pittsburgh, Pennsylvania. My old traveling partner, Mike from the ZooTV Tour, and I drove the five-hour drive from Baltimore to Pittsburgh staying at his grandmother's house. While waiting outside the stadium I met Ken, one of the guys on the crew who drove one of the trucks that carried parts of the elaborate PopMart stage from city to city. Ken was to be a source for a couple cool U2 experiences that tour. Fun Lovin' Criminals opened this show, as they would for all six shows I would see on the first leg of PopMart.

The set list for my first PopMart show in Pittsburgh on May 22, 1997 was as follows: Mofo, I Will Follow, Even Better Than The Real Thing, Gone, Pride, I Still Haven't Found-Stand By Me, Last Night On Earth, Until The End Of The World, If God Will Send His Angels, Staring At The Sun, Sweet Caroline, Miami, Bullet the Blue Sky, Please, Where the Streets Have no Name, Discotheque, If You Wear That Velvet Dress, With or Without You, Hold Me Thrill Me Kiss Me Kill Me, Mysterious Ways, One-Unchained Melody.

U2 show #10 – May 24, 1997 – Columbus

A couple of days later, Mike and I drove three hours from Pittsburgh to Columbus, Ohio for our second PopMart show on May 24, 1997 at Ohio State University. We saw Bono get off the bus, but he was swarmed by fans. It wasn't as orderly as it had been on ZooTV. We got a few pictures though. We also signed the banner hanging outside the stadium. Our seats weren't too close for this show.

The set list for the PopMart show in Columbus on May 24, 1997 was as follows: Mofo, I Will Follow, Even Better Than The Real Thing, Gone, Pride, I Still Haven't Found-Stand By Me, Last Night On Earth, Until The End Of The World, If God Will Send His Angels, Staring At The Sun, Daydream Believer,

Miami, Bullet the Blue Sky, Please, Where the Streets Have no Name, Discotheque, If You Wear That Velvet Dress, With or Without You, Hold Me Thrill Me Kiss Me Kill Me, Mysterious Ways, One.

U2 show #11 – May 26, 1997 – DC

Two days later, Mike and I were at the PopMart show at RFK Stadium in Washington, DC on May 26, 1997. In fact, almost everyone I knew was there since I had gotten most of my friends tickets to the show. It was great! I was in the fifth row from the stage in the center. It rained just as it had at the DC show on the ZooTV tour five years earlier, but this time it really poured. Something about raining in DC for U2 shows. It rained during the U2 show on the Joshua Tree tour, and that is when Bono fell and broke his collarbone. Then it rained again on the ZooTV and PopMart tours. Luckily both the Elevation and Vertigo tours to follow were indoors, so no chance of rain.

The set list for this show was the same as the ones in Pittsburgh and Columbus, except "Unchained Melody" was not played in Columbus, and Edge sang "Sweet Caroline" in Pittsburgh. The set list for the PopMart show in DC on May 26, 1997 was as follows: Mofo, I Will Follow, Even Better Than the Real Thing, Gone, Pride, I Still Haven't Found What I'm Looking For, Last Night on Earth, Until the End of the World, If God Will Send His Angels, Staring at the Sun, Daydream Believer (Edge Karaoke), Miami, Bullet the Blue Sky, Where the Streets Have No Name / Playboy Mansion, Discotheque, If You Wear That Velvet Dress, With or Without You, Hold Me Thrill Me Kiss Me Kill Me, Mysterious Ways, One, Unchained Melody.

U2 show #12 – May 31, 1997 – East Rutherford

My next Popmart show was at Giants Stadium in East Rutherford, New Jersey on May 31. This time my friend Laurie went with me. She wasn't a big U2 fan, but just wanted to go for the experience. I think back then I bugged all of my friends to accompany me to U2 shows. That all ended on the Elevation tour, and I have been going alone ever since. I always meet up with friends at the shows. We had floor seats for this first PopMart show at Giants Stadium. There were three shows, but I only went to the first two. I have no idea why I did not go to the third show.

The set list for this first PopMart show at Giants Stadium in New Jersey on May 31, 1997 was as follows: Mofo, I Will Follow, Gone, Even Better Than The Real Thing, Pride, I Still Haven't Found-Stand By Me, Last Night On Earth, Until The End Of The World, If God Will Send His Angels, Staring At The Sun, Daydream Believer, Miami, Bullet the Blue Sky, Please, Where the Streets Have No Name, Discotheque, If You Wear That Velvet Dress, With or Without You, Hold Me Thrill Me Kiss Me Kill Me, Mysterious Ways-Rain, One.

U2 show #13 – June 1, 1997 – East Rutherford

This may have been my 13th U2 show, but it was a lucky one for me! Unlike the previous night, we did not have close floor seats for this second Popmart show at Giants Stadium. We were way up in the stands on the side of the stage, at least before the show started. Ken, the crew member

I had met at the Pittsburgh show, brought us down to the floor so we could be close to stage for the show.

As Ken was walking us down to the floor, the lights went down indicating it was time for U2 to start the show. Ken had to walk us behind the stage to get to where we were going and at that exact time, U2 was walking out. We stood right at the stairs as Larry, Bono, Edge and Adam walked onto the stage. I was instructed not to scream, but I almost passed out from holding in my excitement. This was the first time I had ever been that close to Larry! It was also at this show that Bono and Edge performed "Staring at the Sun" acoustically for the first time.

The set list for this second PopMart show at Giants Stadium in New Jersey on June 1, 1997 was as follows: Mofo, I Will Follow, Even Better Than The Real Thing, Gone, Pride, I Still Haven't Found-Stand By Me, Last Night On Earth, Until The End Of The World, If God Will Send His Angels-Hallelujah, Staring At The Sun, Sweet Caroline, Miami, Bullet the Blue Sky, Please, Where the Streets Have no Name, Discotheque, If You Wear That Velvet Dress, With or Without You, Hold Me Thrill Me Kiss Me Kill Me, Mysterious Ways, Rain-One-Unchained Melody.

U2 show #14 – June 8, 1997 – Philadelphia

My sixth PopMart show, and final one on that first leg, was on June 8, 1997 at Franklin Field at the University of Pennsylvania in Philadelphia, Pennsylvania. I went to this show with my best friend Cindy. We arrived to see Bono and Larry get off the buses, but like in Columbus they were swarmed by fans and we couldn't get close. I managed to get a couple of pictures though.

The set list for the PopMart show in Philly on June 8, 1997 was as follows: Mofo, I Will Follow, Even Better Than The Real Thing, Gone, Pride, I Still Haven't Found-Stand By Me, Last Night On Earth, Until The End Of The World, If God Will Send His Angels, Staring At The Sun, Daydream Believer, Miami, Bullet the Blue Sky-America, Please, Where the Streets Have No Name, Discotheque, If You Wear That Velvet Dress, With or Without You, Hold Me Thrill Me Kiss Me Kill Me, Mysterious Ways, One-Hallelujah.

My non-U2 show – June 18, 1997 – Oakland

Ken, the U2 crew guy I met in Pittsburgh and who helped me out in Jersey, invited me out to Oakland, California for the U2 show. By this time we were dating, in a long distance kind of way. This was the first and only time I ever dated a roadie or someone on the U2 crew, and I did not do it to get close to U2. I actually liked the guy, although the perks did not hurt. I continued to see Ken after the first leg of the PopMart tour ended. I visited him at his house in Arizona and traveled with him on the tour bus on the Lollapalooza tour when he was the lighting guy for Orbital.

I was at Oakland-Alameda County Stadium on June 18, 1997, but for some reason that escapes me now I did not go to the U2 show. I did get a VIP laminated pass and went back stage. I met Fenton, of *Rattle and Hum*'s "could you pass me a tissue Fenton" fame. He was doing laundry. I assume U2's laundry. Ken and I never went to that U2 show, but we did have a great time exploring all around San Francisco. I would have to wait a few more months for another PopMart show.

U2 show #15 – November 10, 1997 – Tampa

I traveled to Florida for the third leg of U2's PopMart tour. My parents have a condo in Ft. Myers, so I had a free place to stay. My friend Laurie, who's not really a U2 fan but wanted to vacation in Florida, flew down with me to attend the shows in Tampa and Miami, both about a two hour drive from Ft. Myers.

The U2 concert in Tampa, Florida on November 10, 1997 at Houlihans Stadium was my favorite show of the PopMart tour. At the time, it was actually my favorite U2 show I had ever seen, including all of the ZooTV shows. Part of the reason I enjoyed it so much was because I stood right at the B Stage, rather than staying in my seat a few rows back. This was a big deal in the days before we had GA (general admission).

Not only did U2 play a set on the B Stage, they also entered the stadium through the audience and onto the B Stage. Talk about exciting! Opening act Third Eye Blind also made use of the B Stage, and I found the lead singer Stephen Jenkins very appealing. U2 sounded better in Tampa than at the shows I had seen on the first leg of PopMart. Even though it was raining and the top deck of the stadium was empty, it was a great show and a great energy that night!

Instead of karaoke like on the first leg of the tour, Edge sang "Sunday Bloody Sunday" by himself! That night a belly dancer from the audience came on stage for "Mysterious Ways," like during ZooTV. I did not know it at the time, but that belly dancer was Melissa Pruitt who I would meet four years later on the Elevation Tour and has been my friend ever since. Also in attendance that night was a young fan seeing her first U2 show. Her name is Beth Nabi, and I would meet her 14 years later on the 360 Tour, and we have been friends ever since. So in many ways, that U2 PopMart show in Tampa is very significant for me.

The set list for my favorite PopMart show, in Tampa on November 10, 1997, was as follows: Mofo, I Will Follow, Gone, Even Better Than The Real Thing, Last Night On Earth, Until The End Of The World, New Year's Day, Pride, I Still Haven't Found, All I Want Is You, Staring At The Sun, Sunday Bloody Sunday, Bullet the Blue Sky-America, Please, Where the Streets Have No Name, Discotheque, If You Wear That Velvet Dress, With or Without You, Hold Me Thrill Me Kiss Me Kill Me, Mysterious Ways, One-Wake Up Dead Man.

U2 show #16 – November 14, 1997 – Miami, FL

A few days later on November 14, 1997, I was at Pro Player Stadium in Miami for my last PopMart show. Just like the show in Tampa, I again did not stay in my seat and stood right at the B Stage. This time Smashmouth opened, but they were not as exciting as Third Eye Blind. When U2 played their set on the B Stage, Bono leaned into the audience with his leg up on the rail. I grabbed onto Bono's leg, sort of hugged it actually. Although I have always been a Larry fan, I was really digging Bono during PopMart. I think it is the best he has ever looked. Bono's natural color hair was short, and he was in great shape. So yeah, I almost converted and became a "Bono girl" in November of 1997, ALMOST! Don't worry Larry, I still love you the best! It was just a momentary lapse.

The set list was the same in Miami as it was in Tampa, except of course U2 played "Miami" in Miami. The set list for my final PopMart show in Miami on November 14, 1997 was as follows: Mofo, I Will Follow, Gone, Even Better Than The Real Thing, Last Night On Earth, Until The End Of The World,

New Year's Day, Pride, I Still Haven't Found, All I Want Is You, Staring At The Sun, Sunday Bloody Sunday, Miami, Bullet the Blue Sky, Please, Where the Streets, Discotheque, If You Wear That Velvet Dress, With or Without You, Hold Me Thrill Me Kiss Me Kill Me, Mysterious Ways, One-Wake Up Dead Man.

Post PopMart Thoughts

I really enjoyed the PopMart tour. I do not think it gets the credit it deserves. PopMart did not sell out every stadium, but there were some great performances. Edge singing karaoke to either "Sweet Caroline" or "Daydream Believer" on the first leg and "Sunday Bloody Sunday" acoustic solo on the third leg were definitely highlights for me. It was visually pleasing as well. There was a giant golden arch like McDonald's, a giant martini and a giant disco ball traveling lemon that brought Larry, Bono, Edge and Adam to the encore.

PopMart was also the only time I have seen U2 in a uniform of sorts. They each had their own shirt: Bono was "BonoMan," Larry was "HitMan," Adam was "PopTart," and Edge was "Mr. the Edge." I proudly have both a "HitMan" and BonoMan" shirt. PopMart was my favorite look for U2 as a whole. By the end of tour, "If You Wear That Velvet Dress" became one of my favorites off *Pop*. For some reason, "Velvet Dress" was the one song that played in my head after each concert.

My Summer in Dublin, Ireland 1998

The year after PopMart I spent the summer in Dublin, Ireland. Actually it was six weeks. I stayed and studied at Trinity College and took weekend visits to London and Belfast. While in Dublin, I visited the U2 sights. I walked from Trinity to Windmill Lane Studio and saw the wall where all the U2 fans signed, just like the wall at Graceland. I went to Kilmainham Gaol where the video for "A Celebration" was filmed, but they didn't let me on the staircase – just like at Graceland. A running theme in my life seems to be my U2 and Elvis passions intersecting.

While in Dublin, I saw the play *Grease* at the Point Depot Theater where U2 played their famous "go away and dream it all up again" New Year's Eve show in 1989/1990. I went to Bono's house and walked into his backyard, and I went to the hearing aid store, Bono Vox, that Bono was supposedly named after. I even went to U2's night club, The Kitchen, when Howie B was the DJ. I was in Dublin for almost two months, and never saw Larry, Bono, Edge or Adam, but I had one of the best summers of my life!

NetAid – October 9, 1999 – East Rutherford

The following year I drove up to Giants Stadium in East Rutherford, New Jersey on Saturday October 9, 1999 for Net Aid, a benefit concert to raise money and awareness for the Jubilee 2000 campaign to cancel debt in poorer countries. Bono and Wyclef Jean closed the show with their song "New Day," which I was obsessed with and still love to this day. Earlier in the show, Bono performed "One." It would be another year and a half before I would see U2 again.

Elevation

Larry hugging me in Baltimore October 2001
(Photo by Tasha Hindman)

All That You Can't Leave Behind

October 30, 2000 was a preamble to what would be one of the best years of my life, U2001. It was the day *All That You Can't Leave Behind* was released and the wonderful Elevation Tour would follow a few months later. This album could not have come at a better time for Americans as its songs helped comfort them almost a year later on 9/11.

I immediately fell in love with *All That You Can't Leave Behind* at first listen. It instantly became one of my favorite U2 albums. It is my fourth favorite after *The Joshua Tree*, *Rattle and Hum* and *Achtung Baby*. My favorite songs off of *All That You Can't Leave Behind* are "In a Little While," "When I Look at the World," "Beautiful Day," "Walk On" and "Stuck in a Moment You Can't Get Out Of." "In a Little While" is just one of those songs that touches my soul, that gives me goose bumps every time I hear it. But my favorite line off *All That You Can't Leave Behind*, and one of my favorite U2 lyrics ever, comes from "When I Look at the World" – "When your thoughts are too expensive to ever want to keep." I just love that line and being very opinionated with no filter, it gives me a little validity to be that way. U2 won three grammys for "Beautiful Day" – Song of the Year, Record of the Year and Best Rock Performance by a group or duo.

U2 went on the road in support of *All That You Can't Leave Behind* with the Elevation Tour that started and ended in America, more specifically started and ended in Florida. I saw 27 shows on the Elevation tour that spanned from March to December 2001, including the first and final shows of the tour. This was the first time I had ever been to the first and last show of a U2 tour. This was also the first time I went to more than eight shows of a U2 tour. I traveled across the United States from Maryland to Florida to Washington state and back to Florida making great friends along the way. I had a job in sales working from home, which is why I had the flexibility to travel and go to so many U2 shows.

In between the first and third legs of the Elevation Tour on September 11, 2001, the worst terrorist attack on U.S. soil occurred and changed our lives forever. I was actually in New York City just a few days before the Twin Towers fell. I was at the MTV Video Music Awards, outside on the red carpet shaking hands with Bono, Adam and Paul McGuinness (Edge and Larry just waved). A month later, U2 continued the Elevation Tour comforting audiences at this horrific time with songs like "New York," "Grace" and "Peace on Earth." Categorizing *All That You Can't Leave Behind* as timely is an understatement.

U2 show #17 – Elevation Tour Opener - March 24, 2001 – Ft. Lauderdale

I woke up on a bright, sunny Saturday morning in my parents' condo in Ft. Myers, Florida. I left around 9am on March 24, 2001 and drove two hours over to Ft. Lauderdale. Since I had seats, not general admission, before going to the National Car Rental Center for the very first U2 Elevation show, I met my friend Mike (a different Mike from my ZooTV and PopMart friend Mike) at the Orioles Spring Training game. The Orioles won and both my favorites Cal Ripken and Brady Anderson played. It is nice when you can combine U2 shows with sporting events. After the Orioles game, we watched the Maryland Terps NCAA basketball game, which they won sending them to the Final Flour for the first time ever. It was a "Beautiful Day" for sure and was about to be a beautiful night.

At the time, the Elevation Tour Opener was the best U2 show I had ever seen. This would be my reaction after each Elevation show, they just kept getting better and better. Opening Night was truly a great show, mostly because it was the very first show of the tour so I did not know what to expect. The Elevation set list was fantastic, a much better mix of songs than I heard on the ZooTV and PopMart tours. U2 opened with "Elevation," went into "Beautiful Day," and played (not in order) "Bad," "New Year's Day," "Sunday Bloody Sunday," "Gone," "Discotheque," "Staring at the Sun," "Until the End of the World," "Mysterious Ways," "The Fly," "Streets," "With or Without You," "Bullet," "I Will Follow," "Sweetest Thing," "Ground Beneath Her Feet," "New York," "Stuck in a Moment," "In a Little While." U2 closed with "One," but then added "Walk On." I did miss my favorites "I Still Haven't Found What I'm Looking For" and "Pride," but it was an amazing show! I was so excited that "Gone" had remained in the set list from PopMart.

My seat for Opening Night wasn't that great, but not that bad either. I was on the first level pretty much in the back about 12 rows from the floor. Bono spent a lot of time on the catwalk, and he fell off of it. His voice was amazing though. I knew after this show, the Elevation tour would be the best tour ever. I was right. The Elevation tour is still my favorite U2 tour.

The complete set list (in order) for Opening Night of the Elevation Tour in Ft. Lauderdale on March 24, 2001 was as follows: Elevation, Beautiful Day, Until the End of the World, New Year's Day, Stuck In A Moment, Gone, Discotheque-Staring at the Sun, New York, I Will Follow, Sunday Bloody Sunday-Get Up Stand Up, Sweetest Thing, In A Little While, Ground Beneath Her Feet, Bad, Where the Streets Have No Name, Mysterious Ways, The Fly, Bullet the Blue Sky, With or Without You, One, Walk On.

U2 show #18 – March 26, 2001 – Ft. Lauderdale

For the second show of the Elevation Tour on March 26, 2001, I still did not have general admission, but arrived at the National Car Rental Center early anyway with hopes of seeing Bono, and I did! I left the Orioles spring training game early to get to the arena by 3pm to see U2 arrive. After a few minutes of walking around the arena parking lot, I found out where U2 was going to drive in, along with about 20 other people waiting.

Just before 3:30pm, Bono drove in, saw us and walked over to speak with us and sign autographs. Unfortunately people kept circling him and pushing, so I wasn't able to get an autograph or actually speak with Bono one on one. I was basically one person away from him, and I was able to shout out things. Bono asked us if we had been to the show Saturday and if we liked it – uh YES, of course! Bono said "Bad" was very special, and he's glad they worked it in again. Again, YES! so were we! Bono said he thought "Bullet" was the best song of the night. (I am so not a fan of "Bullet the Blue Sky," but kept that to myself.) Bono made a little joke about how he fell off the catwalk. When asked how Ali was feeling, Bono responded "big" (she was pregnant). Too bad I did not have a video camera because that was a great exchange, just like a Bono mini press conference.

The second show of the Elevation Tour did not disappoint. My seat was fabulous, next to the stage and catwalk 15 rows up. The Corrs again opened as they had on Opening Night. The second night differed from opening night in that U2 played "Angel of Harlem" and a little bit of "Unchained Melody" at the end of "One." Unfortunately, "Gone" and "Ground Beneath Her Feet" were left off the set list that night, as was "I Will Follow." Bono sang the Rolling Stones' "Ruby Tuesday" at the end of "Bad." During the band introductions, Bono said Larry was the son and father of Elvis. Once again my U2 and Elvis passions collide. Apparently, Lenny Kravitz was at the show. Ten years later I would see Lenny Kravitz open for U2 on the 360 tour.

The set list for the second Elevation show in Ft. Lauderdale on March 26, 2001 was as follows: Elevation, Beautiful Day, Until the End of the World, Discotheque-Devil Inside-Staring at the Sun, Stuck In a Moment, New York, New Year's Day, Sunday Bloody Sunday-Get Up Stand Up, Sweetest Thing, In A Little While, Angel of Harlem, Bad-Sympathy For the Devil, Where the Streets Have No Name, Mysterious Ways, The Fly, Encore(s): Bullet the Blue Sky, With or Without You, One-Unchained Melody, Walk On.

U2 show #19 – March 29, 2001 – Charlotte

A few days later on my way home to Baltimore, I flew from Ft. Myers, Florida to Charlotte, North Carolina for the U2 show at Charlotte Coliseum on March 29, 2001. Nelly Furtado opened because PJ Harvey cancelled, and I did not like Nelly Furtado at all. This was my first General Admission (GA) U2 show ever. For the ZooTV and PopMart Tours, the shows were seated. For some reason, I got seats for the first two shows of the Elevation Tour. But the third Elevation show, I was GA standing front row at the tip of the heart, which was at the point of the catwalk. It was sort of like standing at the B Stage on PopMart, but better. Bono was literally right in front of me, and he was there for half of the show. After being introduced, Larry walked down and stood right in front of me. It was an amazing show! I loved being that close, obviously. Set changes from the previous two shows were as follows: full band "Staring at the Sun," no "Discotheque," "Ground Beneath Her Feet" was back, no "Angel of Harlem" and still no "Gone" or "I Will Follow," and no "Unchained Melody" at the end of "One."

The set list for the Elevation show in Charlotte on March 29, 2001 was as follows: Elevation, Beautiful Day, Until the End of the World, New Year's Day, Stuck In A Moment, Staring at the Sun, New York, Sunday Bloody Sunday, Sweetest Thing, In A Little While, Ground Beneath Her Feet, Bad, Where the Streets Have No Name, Mysterious Ways, The Fly, Bullet the Blue Sky, With or Without You, One, Walk On.

U2 show #20 – April 12, 2001 – Tacoma

A month later, I flew to Seattle to visit my friend John from high school who was stationed there and to see the U2 show in Tacoma, Washington on April 12, 2001. The day before the U2 show John and I went to the Space Needle, had dinner at a great seafood restaurant then listened to some music at this great Irish pub. The next day, we had lunch at this cute pub before getting in the GA line at the Tacoma Dome around 3pm. We didn't see U2 drive in, but we had a lot of fun with other fans who we ended up standing next to at the concert.

I loved the Elevation show in Tacoma even more than the first three I saw in Ft. Lauderdale and Charlotte. It was a longer show with two encores. Edge's five kids were there, which somehow made it more exciting. John and I stood at the tip of the heart just to the left, along with our new friends from the GA line. There was such an amazing energy at that

Tacoma show that I cried twice. PJ Harvey opened and would open for the rest of the shows on the first leg of the tour. I did not like her this first time in Tacoma, but grew to like her with every show and by June 22nd in New Jersey, I was a PJ Harvey fan. The next morning, John and I saw our picture in the Tacoma newspaper singing in the audience as Bono walked by us singing. The caption read, "Beautiful Day for U2 Fans in Tacoma."

Changes to the show from the first three I saw were as follows: "Pride," "Desire," "Ground Beneath Her Feet," "I Will Follow" and "Unchained Melody" were played; but "Dicsotheque," "Staring at the Sun," "Even Better Than the Real Thing" and "Gone" were not played. The full set list for the Elevation show in Tacoma on April 12, 2001 was as follows: Elevation, Beautiful Day, Until the End of the World, New Year's Day, Stuck In A Moment You Can't Get Out Of, Gone, Even Better Than the Real Thing, New York, I Will Follow, Sunday Bloody Sunday-Get Up Stand Up, The Sweetest Thing, In A Little While, Desire, The Ground Beneath Her Feet, Bad-40, Where The Streets Have No Name, Mysterious Ways, The Fly, Bullet The Blue Sky, With Or Without You, Pride, One-Unchained Melody, Walk On.

U2 show #21 – May 4, 2001 – Lexington

About three weeks later, my roommate Vicki and I flew to Kentucky for the U2 show in Lexington and the Kentucky Derby. Vicki was not a U2 fan, but wanted to go to the Kentucky Derby. We flew into Lexington around 11am on May 4th, the morning of the U2 show. Lexington is a great little town. We went to lunch, shopped a little, then I got in the GA line at Rupp Arena around 2pm. Vicki had a seat, so we met up after the show. Around 4pm, Bono walked out to the GA line and thanked us. He was only out there for a few minutes. I hung out with a bunch of nice people in the GA line.

Even though I was within the first 150 people in line, I still stood at the tip of the heart instead of inside the heart at the front of the stage. It was only my third GA show ever, and I thought the tip of the heart was the best place to stand at a U2 concert. It was probably because of all the interaction with Bono. I touched Bono's hand once, the first time he leaned into the crowd. Then I patted Bono's shoulder as he ran between the catwalk and us. That was the first time I had ever done that.

PJ Harvey opened again. I heard "Kite" and "Stay" for the first time. U2 also played an acoustic version of "Desire," but they did not play "Gone," "Staring at the Sun," "Discotheque" or "Ground Beneath Her Feet." "Pride" was my favorite that night in Kentucky. Bono was much more talkative and much more political than he had been at the previous shows. I finally took my camera into the show, and have never gone to a concert without it since. In my journal after the show, I wrote, "What a night! Best U2 show! I know I write that after each concert, but they get better every time I see them! Tomorrow onto Louisville for the Kentucky Derby!"

The set list for the Elevation show in Lexington, Kentucky on May 4, 2001 was as follows: Elevation, Beautiful Day, Until the End of the World, New Year's Day, Kite, New York, I Will Follow, Sunday Bloody Sunday, Stuck In a Moment, In A Little While, Desire, Stay, Bad/40, Where the Streets Have No Name, Mysterious Ways, The Fly, Bullet the Blue Sky, With or Without You, Pride, One, Walk On.

The morning after the U2 show in Lexington, Vicki and I rented a car and drove to Louisville for the day to go to the Kentucky Derby. What an experience that was! Even though I had grown up in Maryland, I have never been to the

Preakness, so I was not prepared for the craziness that was the Kentucky Derby infield. Drunk people everywhere, some holding really inappropriate signs with different sized holes to measure certain parts of the female anatomy. We tried the Kentucky favorite Mint Julep, but had to throw it out because it was so horrid. We got a great spot for the race right on the fence at the first turn, so that was nice. The part of Louisville where Churchill Downs is located was not a nice area. We were happy to drive back to Lexington after the Kentucky Derby.

U2 show #22 – May 6, 2001 – Pittsburgh

The next morning on May 6th, Vicki flew home and I flew to Pittsburgh for the U2 show. I immediately checked into my hotel and was in the GA line at Mellon Arena by 9:30am. Tired doesn't even begin to describe how I felt, but I had a great time in the GA line that day in Pittsburgh. I met so many great people including Tasha and Frank. We ordered pizza and talked about U2. It was my first all-day GA line experience. Sometime in the afternoon, I almost knocked myself out when I hit my head on one of the metal barriers. It was so embarrassing and really hurt! Everyone saw, and I had to hold ice on it for a while.

That U2 show in Pittsburgh had the best set list and best energy of the six Elevation shows I had seen so far. For the first time, I stood inside the heart (not out at the tip). I was one person back front the rail in front of Bono. PJ Harvey opened the show again. "Gone," "Kite," "Angel of Harlem" and "Sweetest Thing" returned to the set list in Pittsburgh. When U2 started "Gone," I screamed so loud scaring my new friend Tasha and her sister Kelly. It was the first time I had heard

"Gone" since Opening Night in Ft. Lauderdale, and "Gone" is one of my top five favorite songs. Bono blew bubbles during "Walk On," and I touched Bono's hand during "Beautiful Day" when he reached out and sang "touch me." But "Gone" was definitely my highlight of the show.

The set list for the Elevation show in Pittsburgh on May 6, 2001 was as follows: Elevation, Beautiful Day, Until the End of the World, New Year's Day, Stuck In a Moment, Gone, Kite, New York, I Will Follow, Sunday Bloody Sunday, Sweetest Thing, In a Little While, Angel of Harlem, Stay, Bad/All I Want Is You, Where the Streets Have No Name, Mysterious Ways, The Fly, Bullet the Blue Sky, With or Without You, Pride, One, Walk On.

That Pittsburgh show was what really started the magical experience that was the Elevation tour. It was the watershed show on my musical journey. It was the first time I stood inside the heart. It was the first time I waited in the GA line all day. It was the first time I made friends who I continued to hang out with during the tour, traveling to shows together.

U2 show #23 – May 7, 2001 – Columbus

The next morning after the Elevation show in Pittsburgh, I flew to Columbus, Ohio for the U2 show at Nationwide Arena. My head still hurt from where I hit it in Pittsburgh. Looking back I probably had a concussion. I am not exaggerating or being dramatic. I had a terrible headache in Columbus, sitting in the GA line resting. For this show, I went back to my spot standing at the tip of the heart. During "Desire," Bono was literally right in front of me playing his harmonica. He leaned down and I thought he was going to give me his harmonica, but he gave it to the guy right next to me. I really wanted that harmonica! Bono sounded especially great in Columbus. He was doing some amazing things with his voice. "Pride" and "One" were highlights for me. Other memorable songs that night were "Gone," "Kite," "Stay" and "Desire." To be fair, "Pride" and "Gone" are always highlights for me.

The set list for the Elevation show in Columbus on May 7, 2001 was as follows: Elevation, Beautiful Day, Until the End of the World, New Year's Day, Stuck In a Moment, Gone, Kite, New York, I Will Follow, Sunday Bloody Sunday, In a Little While, Desire, Stay, Bad, Where the Streets Have No Name, Mysterious Ways, The Fly, Bullet the Blue Sky, With or Without You, Pride, One, Walk On.

After the show in Columbus that night, I wrote in my journal "I can't imagine what it's going to be like after the tour ends. Obviously I love going to the shows, but it's more than that. It's the feeling of a community, knowing everyone around you feels the same way. I love traveling around and meeting all these great people. It's tiring, but amazing!"

U2 show #24 – June 2, 2001 – Albany

The Elevation show in Albany, New York was not originally part of my U2 tour plans. This was first of many shows I added at the last minute along the way. I flew up to Albany and hung out with Tasha (who I had just met a month earlier at the U2 show in Pittsburgh) and her sister all afternoon outside the Pepsi Arena. I met a bunch of people from the U2 internet community. There was no Facebook or Twitter back then, we just had forums. We saw Bono drive in for the sound check, but he did not stop.

I saw this Elevation show from the seats, on the side of the stage. Here is a little advice. If you are going to get a seat for a U2 show, or any concert for that matter, get a seat on the side of the stage. It is cheaper and closer to the stage. You will pay double or triple for a seat with a full front view of the stage, but those seats are really far away. You can see everything from the side of the stage, and you're so close. Next best thing to GA.

PJ Harvey again opened the show. Bono's voice was rough that night in Albany, apparently he was sick. Maybe that is why there were a lot of changes in the set list. U2 played "Mysterious Ways" after "Until the End of the World." "The Fly" was performed in the first encore. "Unchained Melody" was played after "One." The Beatles' "In My Life" was played before "Stuck in a Moment." Van Morrison's "Gloria" was played after "Desire." I was ecstatic "Gone" was still in the set list! But U2 did not play "New Year's Day," "In a Little While" or "Sweetest Thing."

The complete set list for the Elevation show in Albany on June 2, 2001 was as follows: Elevation, Beautiful Day, Until the End of the World, Mysterious Ways, In My Life / Stuck In a Moment, Kite, Gone, New York, I Will Follow, Sunday Bloody Sunday / Get Up Stand Up, Desire, Stay, Bad / 40, Where the Streets Have No Name, Pride, Bullet the Blue Sky, With or Without You, The Fly, One / Unchained Melody, Walk On.

U2 show #25 – June 3, 2001 – Hartford

The Elevation show in Hartford, Connecticut was another last minute addition to the tour for me. The morning after the show in Albany, Tasha and I drove to Hartford and were in the GA line at the Civic Center by 9:00am. The GA line was inside, which was so comfortable and mellow! I met some more U2 friends, including Michelle who was a fellow Elvis fan, and she and I are still friends today.

At the time, that Hartford show was one of my favorites. There was a great energy and at the same time it was very relaxed. It was my first time standing up front at the rail. I was right in front of Adam and for some reason Tasha stood in front of Edge, even though she is an Adam fan. This was the first show I actively started to try to meet Larry or have some interaction with him. I guess my quest for Larry started in Hartford. I wore my Elvis shirt and had made a sign that read, "I love Elvis almost as much as I love Larry. Can I have your sticks?" I am pretty sure Larry, Adam and Bono saw it as they walked on stage, but nothing came from it – at least not that night.

I was especially into the music that night in Hartford. PJ Harvey again opened the show, and by this time I was really starting to like her. U2 played the same set list as Albany, except "In a Little While" was added and "She's a Mystery to Me" was played after "One," the Rolling Stones' "Wild Horses" and "40" was played after "Bad."

The set list for the Elevation show in Hartford on June 3, 2001 was as follows: Elevation, Beautiful Day, Until the End of the World, Mysterious Ways, In My Life/Stuck In a Moment, Kite, Gone, New York, I Will Follow, Sunday Bloody Sunday/Get Up Stand Up, In A Little While, Desire, Stay, Bad/40, Where the Streets Have No Name, Pride, Bullet the Blue Sky, With or Without You, The Fly, One/She's a Mystery To Me, Walk On.

U2 show #26 – June 8, 2001 – Boston

On June 7th a few days after the show in Albany, I flew up to Boston to attend the last two of four Elevation shows at the Fleet Center. These shows were to be filmed for a concert dvd. I only slept seven hours in two days, but it was so worth it. Those two Elevation shows in Boston were truly magnificent! Each day I waited in the hot sun reflecting off the white concrete in the GA line from 7am to 6pm before each show. I hung out with my friends I had met at previous shows as well as Tasha, who had now become my official U2 concert buddy. I was up front on the rail in front of Adam for both shows. I again wore my Elvis shirt and took my sign I had in Hartford, but again no drumsticks.

The Elevation show on June 8th (known to the fans as Boston3) was great. The crowd went insane when U2 played "11 O'Clock Tick Tock." U2 also played "Ground Beneath Her Feet," "All I Want is You," "Angel of Harlem," and "New Year's Day," but did not play "Bad," "In a Little While" or "Pride."

The set list for the third Elevation show in Boston on June 8, 2001 was as follows: Elevation, Beautiful Day, Until the End of the World, New Year's Day, Stuck In a Moment, Kite, Gone, New York, 11 O'Clock Tick Tock, Sunday Bloody Sunday/Get Up Stand Up, Sweetest Thing, Angel of Harlem, The Ground Beneath Her Feet, All I Want Is You, Where the Streets Have No Name, Mysterious Ways, The Fly, Bullet the Blue Sky, With or Without You, One, Walk On.

U2 show #27 – June 9, 2001 – Boston

The next day was truly the best show of the Elevation Tour at that point. The show in Boston on June 9, 2001 is affectionately known by U2 fans as Boston4 and is pretty famous. What made it so great and so memorable was the incredible set list. U2 played songs they don't normally play like "Party Girl," "Out of Control" and "Even Better Than the Real Thing." Furthermore, the set list was all changed around. "Pride" was played second and then four straight songs of Achtung Baby: "Until the End of the World," "The Fly," "Even Better Than the Real Thing" and "Mysterious Ways." After the show, I found out U2 was supposed to play an acoustic version of my favorite song "I Still Haven't Found What I'm Looking For," but played "Stay" instead.

At the end of the show during "Walk On," a fan charged the stage and a U2 security guy tackled him right in front of us. Then Bono tackled the security guard to let the guy on stage. The guy went on to pick up Bono and twirl him around. During the whole show, Boston Red Sox third baseman Nomar Garciapara was standing behind us. It was a crazy, wonderful night. History has shown that the last show in a series of U2 shows in the same city is usually the best one. And by best, I mean a different set list because when you have been to 27 shows on the same tour, it is nice to have a little variety once in a while. Not that I wouldn't go to 100 U2 shows with the same set list.

The set list for the fourth and final Elevation show in Boston on June 9, 2001 was as follows: Elevation, Pride, Until the End of the World, The Fly, Even Better Than the Real Thing, Mysterious Ways, In My Life/Stuck In A Moment, Kite, Gone, New York, Out of Control, Sunday Bloody Sunday, Desire / Van Morrison's Gloria, Party Girl, Stay, Bad / Allison, Where the Streets Have No Name, Beautiful Day, Bullet the Blue Sky, With or Without You, One / She's a Mystery To Me, Walk On.

U2 show #28 – June 11, 2001 – Philadelphia

Barely two days after that fantastic Elevation show in Boston, I woke up at 5:30am on June 11th, drove two hours to Philadelphia, and was in the GA line at First Union Center by 8:10am. It was a long, hot day in the sun, but my U2 family grew as I made many new friends. And of course Tasha was right there with me.

Once inside, I stood up front at the rail just to the right of Adam. PJ Harvey again opened, and by this point I was really loving her performances. We brought cut out paper fish for her song "Down By the Water." She was very excited, and said she didn't know the fish traveled from Boston. Other then the addition of "In a Little While" and a bit of "Night and Day" after "Beautiful Day," it was a standard set list that night in Philly.

The highlight of the night for me was a "Larry Mullen Band" shirt thrown onto the stage. Larry placed it on his drum kit where it stayed for the rest of the show. I found out later that Paola, whom I had yet to meet, had thrown this shirt onto the stage. It was her birthday, and she is a huge Larry fan. She had made the shirt for him. I took pictures of Paola's "Larry Mullen Band" shirt on Larry's drum kit and posted them in one of the U2 forums online. Jenny, who I had met in the GA line in Philly, saw my picture and contacted Paola because it was her shirt. Then the four of us (Tasha, Jenny, Paola and myself) became friends. That is pretty much how the U2 family grows. Paola made us all "Larry Mullen Band" shirts, which we still wear today. I have since made my own "Larry Mullen Band" shirts, which is basically my U2 concert uniform.

The set list for the first Elevation show in Philadelphia on June 11, 2001 was as follows: Elevation, Beautiful Day/Night and Day, Until the End of the World, Mysterious

Ways/Sexual Healing, In My Life/Stuck In a Moment, Kite, Gone, New York, I Will Follow, Sunday Bloody Sunday/Get Up Stand Up, In a Little While, Desire/Gloria, Stay, Bad/40, Where the Streets Have No Name, Pride, Bullet the Blue Sky, With or Without You, The Fly, One, Walk On.

U2 show #29 – June 12, 2001 – Philadelphia

The next morning, I was back in the GA line at 7:30am. Luckily at the time Tasha lived in Philadelphia, so we stayed at her place in between these two shows. Unfortunately Tasha had classes, so she was unable to hang out with us during the day. Around 3pm, we went over where U2 would drive into the arena with hopes of meeting them. There were only about 10 of us waiting, so we thought there was a pretty good chance they would stop.

Around 3:40, a car drove in and stopped right in front of us. Edge got out of the car! I had never met Edge before. We respectfully asked if he would sign autographs, and Edge graciously said, "Yes." Feeling a bit greedy, we then asked if he would take pictures with us. Edge said he wouldn't pose with us, but we could "snap away." I was the second person he came to. I asked him to sign my scrapbook, and he signed the upper left hand corner. I thought to myself, now the others will have to sign the remaining three corners, which has still not happened. Edge did not say much, but he was very nice and stayed until he had signed everyone's stuff.

Later, Paul McGuinness and PJ Harvey drove in, then Larry and Adam. They did not stop. Bono drove in just about 4:45, and he stopped. But by then, there were at least 30 people with us most of whom started screaming and swarming around Bono. He signed a few autographs and took a few pictures before leaving after about two minutes. Bono said he wasn't feeling well, and he looked really out of it.

This second show in Philly was better than the previous night, and at the time it was my favorite so far. Tasha and I stood up front at the rail between Bono and Adam, which had become our usual spot. Luckily for us everyone wants to stand in front of Bono and Edge, so Adam's side is much less crowded. Tasha is an Adam fan, so it worked out perfectly. And I am obviously a Larry fan, so it doesn't really matter where I stand because Larry is in the back. Before the show, I was trying to get Sammy's (Larry's drum tech) attention to get drum sticks, but my voice was shot, so Tasha yelled. Sammy looked at us, and we motioned as if we were playing drums and he sort of nodded.

U2 played "In a Little While," my favorite off *All You Can't Leave Behind* on the main stage right in front of us. Usually it was played acoustically with Edge and Bono at the tip of the hear. This was the best version of "In a Little While" I had ever heard! Bono sang a verse of "Stuck in a Moment" right to Tasha and I! Before "One," about five of us held up a "Jubilee 2000" banner. Bono saw it, was excited and wanted it, so we handed it to him. I touched his hand. It's good to have long arms.

The set list was a little different at that second Elevation show in Philly. U2 played "Mysterious Ways" earlier and "Stuck in a Moment" later than they had been. "All I Want is You," "New Year's Day," and an amazing version of "Ground Beneath Her Feet" were played. U2 also included covers of "In My Life" and "Gloria." But some of my favorites like "Gone," "Bad" and "Pride" were not played. After the show, Tasha yelled to Sammy again. He walked right over to me telling the security guard to make sure I got the drum stick, but I leaned over far enough to take it from him. Again, it is good to have long arms. Sammy gave the other drum stick to Tasha.

The complete set list for the second Elevation show in Philadelphia on June 12, 2001 was as follows: Elevation, Beautiful Day, Until the End of the World, New Year's Day, Kite, New York, I Will Follow, Sunday Bloody Sunday / Get Up Stand Up, Stuck in a Moment, In a Little While, The Ground Beneath Her Feet, Desire / Gloria, All I Want Is You, Where The Streets Have No Name, Mysterious Ways, The Fly, Bullet the Blue Sky, With or Without You, One, Walk On.

U2 show #30 – June 14, 2001 – DC

Two days later on June 14th, U2 played in my hometown at the MCI Center in Washington, DC. Well, not exactly my hometown as I am from Ellicott City, Maryland about 40 miles away but at least I was sleeping in my own bed for those two Elevation shows.

I honestly do not remember too much about the actual songs of the concert because I was sick at this first DC show, but I do remember two distinct moments I had with Bono during the show. I was standing at the tip of the heart because I had been too sick to fight for a spot up front at the rail at the main stage inside the heart. U2 was playing "Desire" out on the tip of the heart in front of me. I was just in awe of being THAT close to Larry. And when I'm sick and tired, my emotions are even that much more heightened. So I completely froze when after "Desire," Bono looked down at me and asked, "What do they sing in DC?" Then Bono sang "Ground Beneath Her Feet" to the girl three down from me. When he messed up one of the lines, I laughed, and Bono looked at me and smiled.

The set list for the first Elevation show in DC on June 14, 2001 was as follows: Elevation, Beautiful Day, Until the

End of the World, Mysterious Ways, Kite, Gone, New York, I Will Follow, Sunday Bloody Sunday / Get Up Stand Up, Stuck In a Moment, In a Little While, Desire / Gloria, The Ground Beneath Her Feet, Bad / Wild Horses / 40, Where the Streets Have No Name, Pride, Bullet the Blue Sky, With or Without You, One, Walk On.

U2 show #31 – June 15, 2001 – DC

The next day for the second Elevation show in DC, I did not spend much time in the GA line. Instead I hung out with my new friends Jennifer and John in the Discovery Store and Ruby Tuesday's near the GA line. Somehow, we got up front and stood at the rail in front of Adam. That second show in DC had a really great energy and at the time I thought it was up there with Boston4 and Philly2. U2 played "11 O'Clock Tick Tock," "Sweetest Thing," "New Year's Day," and "All I Want is You." "Gone and "Bad" were not played. PJ Harvey again opened these shows.

The set list for the second Elevation show in DC on June 15, 2001 was as follows: Elevation, Beautiful Day, Until the End of the World, New Year's Day, Stuck In a Moment, Kite, New York, 11 O'Clock Tick Tock, Sunday Bloody Sunday / Get Up Stand Up, Sweetest Thing, Desire, Stay, All I Want Is You, Where the Streets Have No Name, Mysterious Ways, The Fly, Bullet the Blue Sky, With or Without You, Pride, One, Walk On / Hallelujah.

U2 show #32 – June 21, 2001 – East Rutherford

Less than a week later, I drove up to East Rutherford, New Jersey for the end of the first leg of the Elevation Tour. I left around 6:30pm Wednesday night June 20th the night before the U2 show and met Tasha at the hotel around 10pm. We got up early the next morning and were in the GA line at Continental Airlines Arena by 6:15am. I was number 30 in line. Tasha tried all day to get a GA, but couldn't so she stayed in her seat behind the stage. I again stood at the rail in front of Adam. PJ Harvey opened these last shows as she had every Elevation show since the fourth one.

It is funny. I do not remember one thing about the songs of the concert that first night in Jersey. All I remember is my very first Larry Mullen Jr. encounter, which made Jersey1 on June 21st one of my favorite all-time U2 shows! A girl two people down from me had a sign that read, "Larry may I please have your drum sticks?" At the end of the show right after "Walk On," Larry hopped up and walked right over to her. I took a great close up picture as Larry leaned over to give her his drum stick. Then Larry looked right into my eyes and nodded. I leaned further than anyone. Larry gave me his drum stick. I mouthed, "Thank You So Much." Larry again nodded.

As soon as I got Larry's drum stick, I began to tear up. I looked up at Tasha in her seat behind the stage as she has witnessed the entire interaction, and we both started jumping up and down. Then I just walked back into the middle of the heart by myself and started to cry and shake. At the time, that was the best moment of the tour for me! I exited the arena clutching my drum stick that Larry gave me. I met up with Tasha outside, and we hugged and told her the story. I could not get to sleep until about 2:30am replaying Larry giving me his drum stick over and over in my head.

The set list for the first Elevation show in Jersey on June 21, 2001 was as follows: Elevation, Beautiful Day, Until the End of the World, Mysterious Ways, Kite, Gone, New York, I Will Follow, Sunday Bloody Sunday / Get Up Stand Up, In My Life / Stuck In a Moment, In a Little While, Desire, Stay, Bad / Wild Horses / 40, Where the Streets Have No Name, Pride, Bullet the Blue Sky, With or Without You, The Fly, One, Walk On.

U2 show #33 – June 22, 2001 – East Rutherford

After only two hours of sleep and still on my high from Larry handing me his drum stick, we were back in the GA line by 5am at Continental Airlines Arena for the final show on the first leg of the Elevation Tour. I was number 14 this time. Tasha and I went over around 3:30pm to wait for U2 to come in, but at 5:15 they had not yet arrived and we had to get back into the GA line. If we missed the final call, we would risk losing our great spot for the concert, which at number 14 in line was sure to be up front and center. After the concert, I found out Larry arrived five minutes after we left and signed autographs and took pictures with everyone who was waiting. I did get to stand up front at the rail almost dead center about two people to the right of Bono's microphone. It was a great spot for the show, but I would have rather met Larry that day.

That regret aside, Jersey2 on June 22nd was an absolutely amazing show! U2 played "Wild Honey" for the first time, and it was an acoustic version with Bono and Edge at the tip of the heart with U2 producer Daniel Lanois playing guitar on the main stage. Daniel Lanois also played with U2 on "Ground Beneath Her Feet." Bono finally sang the extra verse to "With or Without You," "we'll shine like stars in the summer night…" I got Adam's fake pick from Dallas (Edge's guitar tech), the decorative Elevation Tour pick, not the one he actually used. I made a sign that simply read, "Thank You Larry!" I held it up as U2 walked on stage, and Larry nodded. Then I held it up at the end of "Beautiful Day" and Larry nodded and smiled. After the show, I held up my sign again and patted my heart, Larry saw and smiled and nodded again then walked off the stage. I was such an emotional mess at the end of this show.

Tasha and I decided to wait for U2 after the show. We thought we saw Larry leave around 1:30am, but we couldn't really tell if it was him in the car, so we kept waiting. By 3:30am, Tasha and I were the only ones left outside the arena. Not sure why we were still waiting. I think we were in denial about the tour ending. After being up for 24 hours, we finally went back to the hotel to sleep.

The set list for the final show of the first leg of the Elevation tour in Jersey on June 22, 2001 was as follows: Elevation, Beautiful Day, Until the End of the World, New Year's Day, Kite, New York, I Will Follow, Sunday Bloody Sunday / Get Up Stand Up, In My Life / Stuck In a Moment, In a Little While, Desire, Wild Honey, The Ground Beneath Her Feet, Bad / Everybody Hurts / 40, Where the Streets Have No Name, Mysterious Ways / Sexual Healing, The Fly, Bullet the Blue Sky, With or Without You, Pride, One, Walk On / Hallelujah.

MTV Video Music Awards – September 6, 2001 – New York City

At the time, I wrote in my journal that the night of VMAs in New York City on September 6, 2001 was "Arguably the best night of my life." Tasha and I were in New York City at the Metropolitan Opera House standing right at the rope on the red carpet for the MTV Video Music Awards. We were diagonally behind the MTV News desk. We had signed up to be seat fillers for the VMAs, but we did not get into the awards show, rather on the red carpet for the arrivals.

Jennifer Lopez arrived first, but the first person I was excited to see was Chris Kattan from *Saturday Night Live*. We kept shouting "Mango" and he waved. Then we saw Will Ferrell from *Saturday Night Live*. We cheered for him and said we liked his pants and he interacted with us. We then saw Fatboy Slim and nobody else knew who he was. We wished him luck and he waved and thanked us. We then got VERY excited for Jon Bon Jovi and Richie Sambora, especially Tasha. They smiled and waved at us.

It was 8:45pm and still no sign of U2, and we were getting a little worried. Then all of a sudden, I saw Larry down at the other end of the red carpet. I began SCREAMING! Then I saw Adam, and then Bono and Edge. Larry was the first to make his way to us. I lost it! Blowing kisses, holding my heart, screaming, pretty much making a fool of myself. He smiled and waved at me, but kept walking. Edge then came toward us and smiled and waved, but kept walking. Paul McGuinness was walking on our side of the rope, so we thanked him. He looked at us sort of strangely, then he smiled. Tasha shook his hand, and I patted him on his back. Then all of a sudden, Adam was on our side of the rope as well, and he wasn't supposed to be. He tripped on the red carpet and almost fell. We shouted his name, so he turned around. For some reason, I was holding Adam's hand. He was kind of bent over as if he was limbo-ing the rope. Adam had this goofy look on his face acting like he was going to fall. Then Bono walked right up to us and over the rope to shake our hands. It was absolutely amazing! We then watched as John Norris interviewed U2.

After the pre-show was over, we went to this bar called O'Connor's (or something like that) on 64th Street and Columbus to watch the VMAs. U2 did not win any of the five categories they were nominated in, but they did perform "Elevation" and "Stuck in a Moment You Can't Get Out Of." After the show, we took the train back to Jersey, then I drove home and was asleep by 5am. Five days later was 9/11.

U2 show #34 – October 19, 2001 – Baltimore

Just over a month later I started the third leg of the Elevation Tour in my hometown of Baltimore, and this time it really was my hometown show. I was going to the next eight consecutive Elevation shows. The U2 show at the Baltimore Arena on October 19, 2001 started my mini-tour off with a bang. It was absolutely amazing! At the time it was the best I had seen out of ZooTV, PopMart and the first leg of Elevation, and it is still one of my favorite shows today!

Our adventure started the night before the show when Jennifer, John, Tasha, Dan, Jenny and myself met at a restaurant in downtown Baltimore near the Baltimore Arena to celebrate Tasha's birthday. After, we drove by the arena to check out the GA line. There were already about 50 people in line at 10:30pm. Jenny and Dan got in line while the rest of us went back to my apartment about 20 minutes away to get our stuff. We were all in the GA line by 1:30am. We had so much fun hanging out with everyone, but it was really cold. Tasha and I slept in my car in the parking garage for about an hour to warm up a little.

Around 3pm, we went over to wait for U2 to arrive. Around 4:30, U2 finally drove in and parked right inside the arena. Then much to our surprise one by one they each walked out to greet us. This was the first time U2 had ever played Baltimore, so I guess they wanted to spend time with the fans taking pictures and signing autographs. There were a lot of us there, but we were behind barricades. Luckily Tasha and I were up front on the barricade, actually pressed up against it. Bono was the first to come over to us as we were sort of in the middle of the line. Then Adam came over and Tasha could barely contain herself. Adam signed Tasha's purple camouflage pants she was wearing in his honor as she told him. Adam said, "They're great ones." I got all of this on video.

When Larry came one person away from me, his bodyguard (David Guyer) told me to turn off my video camera. So I did not get video of my encounter with Larry, but Tasha took a great picture of it and I still remember it like it was yesterday. Larry walked over to me. I said, "I don't have anything for you to sign, so can I have a hug?" Larry looked at me a little strange, then smiled and said yes. Then we hugged and it was a nice, strong hug. In the picture, Larry has a big smile on his face. After the hug, I thanked him. Tasha hugged me and then I cried like a baby. I was so overcome with emotion. I had been waiting to meet Larry for 14 years! I have no idea how I missed Edge, but it was ok since I had met him in Philadelphia.

The Elevation concert in Baltimore was so amazing! It was just one month after 9/11, so you can imagine how emotional it was. We stood at the tip of the heart. Garbage was supposed to open the show, but their drummer got sick, so Graham Parker & the Figgs filled in at the last minute before heading over to their own show at a nearby club. As soon as the Beatles' "All You Need is Love" came on, the crowd went wild, and even crazier for "St. Pepper's." And then we were Elevated, "WOO HOO!" During "New Year's Day," we held up an American Flag. Bono took it from us and hugged it.

Bono looked at me and said, "You take it back," and he handed it back to me so gently. Bono said, "Thank you." I said, "Thank you." Bono started walking away, turned to me, gave me the peace sign and nodded. That was probably the best Bono concert moment I have ever had!

My favorite songs of the night were "I Still Haven't Found What I'm Looking For" (I cried), "Pride" (with MLK's speech a la ZooTV), "Out of Control," "Staring at the Sun" and "Please" (first time played on the tour). A guy behind us was pulled up on stage to play "Knocking on Heaven's Door" with U2. During "One," all of the names of the passengers on the flights from 9/11 were displayed. This was directly followed by "Peace on Earth." I cried through all of this. U2 ended the show with "Walk On." It was the most emotional, spiritual and uplifting U2 show ever, unforgettable!

The set list for the Elevation show in Baltimore on October 19, 2001 was as follows: Elevation, Beautiful Day, Until the End of the World, New Year's Day, Out of Control, Sunday Bloody Sunday, When Will I See You Again / Stuck In a Moment, Kite, Angel of Harlem (full band-electric), Knockin' On Heaven's Door (full band), Staring at the Sun (acoustic), Please, Where the Streets Have No Name, I Still Haven't Found What I'm Looking For, Pride, Bullet the Blue Sky, What's Going On, New York, One, Peace On Earth / Walk On.

U2 show #35 – October 24, 2001 – New York City

A few days later, I began my Elevation road trip seeing seven U2 shows in ten days. This was my first substantial trip on the road with U2. On October 24, 2001, Tasha and I arrived in New York City for the first of three Elevation shows at Madison Square Garden. We took the train up from New

Jersey and were in the GA line by 5:15am, numbers 39 and 40 in line. I was VERY excited to see Macy's just a block away. Not sure why except it was coming up on the Christmas season and one of my favorite Christmas movies is *Miracle on 34th Street*. Around 9am, we saw Sammy and Dallas walk in. Later on in the day, I saw Chris Meloni (Ellicott Stabler from *Law and Order: SVU*) walk out of Penn Station. I love Stabler!

After a stressful GA line procedure, we managed to get great spots up front at the rail between Bono and Adam. Garbage opened. The show had the same set list as the Baltimore show a few days earlier, except U2 played "Bad" instead of "Please." During "Kite," when the spotlight shone on Larry, I screamed, clapped, jumped and down. Larry looked at me, nodded and smiled. Yeah, sadly that is all it takes for me. Our friend Dan got pulled up on stage during "Stuck in a Moment." Our friend Ruth got pulled up on stage and played guitar and sang "Knockin' on Heaven's Door" with U2. All the policemen and firemen who died on 9/11 were listed on the screens during "One." We hung out a bit with everyone after the show, then Tasha and I took the train back to Princeton, then drove back to Tasha's place in Philadelphia.

The set list for the first Elevation show in New York City on October 24, 2001 was as follows: Elevation, Beautiful Day, Until the End of the World, New Year's Day, Out of Control, Sunday Bloody Sunday, Stuck In a Moment, Kite, Angel of Harlem (full band – electric), Knockin' On Heaven's Door (full band), Staring at the Sun (B&E – acoustic), Bad / 40, Where the Streets Have No Name, I Still Haven't Found What I'm Looking For, Pride, Bullet the Blue Sky, What's Going On, New York, One, Peace On Earth / Walk On.

U2 show #36 – October 25, 2001 – New York City

For the second Elevation show at Madison Square Garden in New York City on October 25, 2001, Tasha and I had seats. It was quite relaxing not to have to wait in line all day and stress out about a getting a good 'spot,' but then we realized being in the GA line was half of the fun. We got to MSG early to buy shirts, programs and eat dinner. Our seats were behind/side stage between Adam and Larry, which was perfect for us. No Doubt opened. The set list was actually a little different. U2 played "I Will Follow" instead of "Out of Control," "Stay" instead of "Staring at the Sun," and "Unchained Melody" instead of "Peace on Earth." After the show, we again took the train back to Princeton and then drove back to Tasha's in Philadelphia.

The set list for the second Elevation show in New York on October 25, 2001 was as follows: Elevation, Beautiful Day, Until the End of the World – Two Tribes, New Year's Day, I Will Follow, Sunday Bloody Sunday, When Will I See You Again – Stuck In a Moment, Kite, Angel of Harlem, Stay, Bad – 40, Where the Streets Have No Name, I Still Haven't Found What I'm Looking For, Pride, Bullet the Blue Sky, What's Going On, New York, One – Unchained Melody, Walk On.

U2 show #37 – October 27, 2001 – New York City

We had a day off between the second and third Elevation shows in New York City, so while our friends were in the GA line Tasha and I drove over to New Jersey and checked into our hotel, which we kept through the Elevation show in Jersey on October 28, 2001. On the morning of the last Elevation show at Madison Square Garden on October

27, 2001, we took a bus from Jersey into the City arriving in the GA line around 7am. This GA line was even more stressful than the first, but somehow we ended up at the front rail in front of Adam. Stereophonics opened.

This third Elevation show was definitely the best out of the three in New York City. The set list was pretty much the same, except U2 played "Please" acoustic as well as "Bad." The highlight of the night was when Bono pulled our friend Jenny up at the tip of the heart during "New York" and kissed her on the lips. It was great because Jenny has been a U2 fan since 1981 and nothing like that had ever happened to her. But the truly inspiring part of the night was during "Walk On" when Bono had the FDNY come on stage. They shook hands, the firefighters spoke, Bono sang with his firefighter hat and FDNY shirt on. Bono led them around the heart. U2 closed the show with "Out of Control" with the firefighters still on stage. It was an absolutely amazing experience. So moving just over a month after 9/11!

The set list for the third Elevation show in New York City on October 27, 2001 was as follows: Elevation, Beautiful Day, Until the End of the World, New Year's Day, I Will Follow, Sunday Bloody Sunday, When Will I See You Again / Stuck In a Moment, Kite, Angel of Harlem (full band – electric), Please (Bono, Edge, Bruce Brody), Bad / 40, Where the Streets Have No Name, I Still Haven't Found What I'm Looking For, Pride, Bullet the Blue Sky, What's Going On (Bono, Edge, Larry), New York, One, Peace On Earth / Walk On, Out of Control.

U2 show #38 – October 28, 2001 – East Rutherford

Immediately after the third Elevation show in New York City, Tasha, Paola and I drove to the Continental Airlines Arena to get our numbers in the GA line for the next U2 show the following day on October 28, 2001. This was Paola's first time in General Admission, so she wanted a good spot. I was number 46 in line, the night before the show. We went back to our hotel to sleep and were back in the GA line by 7am the morning of the show. It was a very relaxing GA line. It was nice to be back in East Rutherford, New Jersey where U2 had played two shows to end the first leg of the tour in June, and where Larry had given me his drum stick.

Around 3pm, we walked over to wait for U2 to arrive. We waited until 5:15, but U2 never came. There was chaos when we returned to the GA line. The idiot security people opened up three gates, so those of us who had been waiting all day were right next to people who had just arrived. And all three lines were to go through one door. Sensing severe danger, we decided to get out of the so-called line and go back to wait for the band to arrive and just go into the show later. We should have just stayed where we were waiting for the band. Unfortunately, while dealing with all that line chaos, we missed Bono and Edge by about 10 minutes. But we did arrive in time to see Paul McGuinness, but he was too mobbed to talk to. Lesson learned and why I no longer spend all day waiting in the GA line.

We went into the show after 7pm, leisurely went to the bathroom, got a snack, and watched the show from the soundboard. It was surprisingly close, not a bad view at all. Stereophonics opened. Jersey was not so great to me the second time around, but that was ok because the next shows in Providence would more than make up for it.

The set list for the Elevation show in Jersey on October 28, 2001 was as follows: Elevation, Beautiful Day, Until the End of the World, New Year's Day, I Will Follow, Sunday Bloody Sunday, Stuck In a Moment, Kite, Angel of Harlem (full band – electric), Please (acoustic – Bono, Edge, and guest), All I Want Is You, Where the Streets Have No Name, I Still Haven't Found What I'm Looking For, Pride, Bullet the Blue Sky, What's Going On, New York, One, Peace on Earth / Walk On.

U2 show #39 – October 30, 2001 – Providence

The morning after the U2 Elevation show in New Jersey on October 28, I drove up to Providence, Rhode Island for two shows on October 30 and 31, the second being Larry's 40th Birthday show and my most anticipated show of the tour. I was in the GA line at Dunkin Donuts Center by 3:30pm on October 29th, the day before the first show. I was number 12 in line.

Around 9pm, I went up to my hotel room to eat then went back to the GA line until around 11:30pm. My friends and I went back up to my hotel room to watch U2 on *Late Night with David Letterman*. U2 played "New York" and "Stuck in a Moment," then Bono was interviewed, just Bono. I slept in my room until about 5:30am and then got back in the GA line. Paola flew in around noon. We went to the mall for lunch and then waited for U2 to arrive, but they didn't arrive until after we had gone inside the arena. We did listen to a bit of the techs' sound check through the wall.

The person I went to for a GA wristband was a little slow, so I didn't quite get the spot up front at the rail that I wanted. I was number 12 in line and had been waiting since 3:30pm the day before, so I should have been front and center. I ended up a bit too far to the right, but I was right in front of Adam. Paola was excited because it was her first time inside the heart up front at the rail. Stereophonics opened.

During "Out of Control" when Bono introduced Larry, I of course went nuts screaming and jumping up and down. Bono's security guard John motioned to me, then said something to one of the other guards. A bit later, John came over to read my shirt, "The Larry Mullen Band. It's All About Drums." He smiled and gave me the set list. The only difference to this set list from earlier shows was "When Will I see You Again" was played before "Walk On." Immediately after the show, we got right back in the GA line for the next night because it was going to be Larry's 40th Birthday show.

The set list for the first Elevation show in Providence on October 30, 2001 was as follows: Elevation, Beautiful Day, Until the End of the World, New Year's Day, Out of Control, Sunday Bloody Sunday, Stuck In a Moment, Kite, Angel of Harlem, Please (acoustic), Bad, Where the Streets Have No Name, I Still Haven't Found What I'm Looking For, Pride, Bullet the Blue Sky, What's Going On, New York, One, When Will I See You Again, Walk On.

U2 show #40 – October 31, 2001 Larry Mullen's 40th Birthday – Providence – my favorite concert ever!

Immediately following the first concert in Providence on October 30th, Paola and I got in the GA line for Larry's 40th

Birthday concert the next day. I was number seven in line. Tasha had driven up and met us after the show. We got some food, then Tasha slept in the hotel while Paola and I slept outside in the GA line. Even though it was 30 degrees on that cold sidewalk in Providence in late October, we actually got about five hours of sleep.

We woke up at 8am the morning of October 31st. We went up to our warm hotel room for a couple hours and had some breakfast. We stayed in the GA line all day without leaving, except to take a shower around 3:30pm. I made a huge orange (my favorite color) Birthday Card for Larry and had everyone in the GA line sign it. I put my name and email address on the back just in case. I was optimistic back then, and maybe a little delusional. I had also brought an Elvis motorcycle shirt to give to Larry as a birthday present.

Tasha, Paola and I wore our "Larry Mullen Band" shirts standing up front at the rail between Bono and Adam. I held up the birthday card for Larry as U2 walked on stage, but I don't think Larry saw it. There were many signs that night including one saying, "Bono let Larry sing," but that did not happen. During "Elevation," Bono sang, "Celebration" then said, "Happy Birthday." After "Stuck in a Moment," Larry's 40th birthday celebration began.

Bono led the audience in a chorus of "Happy Birthday" to Larry. Then a birthday cake was brought out, and Larry pretended to throw it out into the audience. Bono said, "Larry likes chocolate cake." Larry took the microphone and came to the front of the stage to talk while Bono sat behind the drums. Larry said, "Bono can't play the drums" then continued with "It took me 40 years to get up front. I'm glad I'm spending my birthday with 18,000 of my closest friends. I feel like I could borrow money from you." Bono asked for a bottle of champagne, which he shook up a la ZooTV and sprayed the audience. Edge took a swig, then Larry drank and continued to drink for the next few songs.

After "Kite," Larry got off the drums and made a B line for me. I got my card and shirt in hand so I could give it to him, but that's not why he was there. Larry gave me his champagne bottle, with champagne still in it! I drank some and shared it with Paola and Tasha, then just hugged the bottle until the security guard offered to put it down behind the barricade until the show ended. I didn't want to let it out of my hands, but sensible thoughts prevailed. I couldn't believe it! Larry wanted to share his birthday with ME! He wanted ME to have a drink on his birthday! I was SO excited I didn't even know U2 changed the set list and played "Wild Honey." I thought it was "Staring at the Sun" as in the past shows. I didn't really come around until "Please."

After "Pride," Larry came back over to me so I could give him the birthday card and Elvis shirt. I said, "Thank you. Happy Birthday." He smiled and said, "Thank You." It wasn't much of a conversation, but it was very meaningful as Larry looked into my eyes just as he had in Jersey when he gave me his drum stick a few months prior. Paola gave Larry her Larry scrapbook, which contained the picture of Larry hugging me in Baltimore a couple weeks earlier. Later on, Bono noticed our "Larry Mullen Band" shirts, shook his head and smiled. I am pretty sure we were the first to have "Larry Mullen Band" shirts. It wasn't until the Vertigo tour that U2 wore "Larry Mullen Band" shirts on stage, and now many fans wear them. Before leaving the stage Larry took Michelle's Elvis sunglasses with sideburns and put them on. I was so elated after the show, just walking around hugging Larry's champagne bottle.

The set list for the Larry's 40th Birthday show in Providence on October 31, 2001 was as follows: Elevation, Beautiful Day, Until the End of the World, New Year's Day, I

Will Follow, Sunday Bloody Sunday, Stuck in a Moment, Happy Birthday Larry, Party Girl, Slow Dancing, Kite, Wild Honey, Please, Bad / 40, Where the Streets Have No Name, I Still Haven't Found What I'm Looking For, Pride, Bullet the Blue Sky, What's Going On, New York, One, When Will I See You Again, Walk On

This show was not only my favorite Elevation show, but my favorite U2 show ever. I doubt there will ever be another night like it. Granted it was Larry's 40th Birthday, and I love Larry, but it was also fantastic for the rarities U2 played that night. "Slow Dancing" was played for the first time on the Elevation Tour, and only the 11th time ever. "Party Girl" and "Wild Honey" were played for the first time on that leg of Elevation, and I have only heard those songs a couple of times ever. There was a great energy in Providence that night. I still have that champagne bottle on my shelf, next to Larry's drum stick he gave me in Jersey. I find it interesting that my 40th U2 show was Larry's 40th Birthday show. Coincidence or fate?

U2 show #41 – November 2, 2001 – Philadelphia

Still on a high from the previous night, sharing champagne with Larry on his 40th birthday at my most favorite U2 show ever, Tasha and I left Providence for Philadelphia. We arrived at the First Union Center at 4:30pm the day before the Elevation show on November 2, 2001. We got our numbers in the GA line, 21 and 22, and then went for dinner, got our pictures developed from the Providence shows, and got snacks for the GA line. By 9:30pm we were back in the GA line and the rest of our friends had arrived. We slept in my car for about three hours and took a shower in a friend's hotel room. That GA line in Philly was the most organized and relaxing line ever. It was quite warm for a November day, which was a welcome change after the cold in Providence. It was a "Beautiful Day" all around.

We got our usual spots up front at the rail in front of Adam. Stereophonics opened again. Tasha wore her "Adam Clayton Band" shirt, and I of course wore my "Larry Mullen Band" shirt. We showed Sammy and Stu (Adam's bass tech). Sammy seemed very excited. I held up my "Larry thanks for the drink" sign as U2 walked on stage. Larry saw it and gave me the Fonzie thumbs up with a smile.

The set list was pretty much the same as it had been, except U2 played "Out of Control" and "Peace on Earth." Of course I went nuts when Bono introduced Larry during "Out of Control." At the end of the show when they were all waving, Larry looked at me, smiled and nodded. After the show, we all met out front to take a group picture. We tried waiting for U2, but they had already left. Some of our friends were sad because it was their last Elevation show and our last time together. But Tasha, Paola, Jenny and I would reunite in a month for the final two shows of the tour in Florida.

The set list for the Elevation show in Philly on November 2, 2001 was as follows: Elevation, Beautiful Day, Until the End of the World, New Year's Day, Out of Control, Sunday Bloody Sunday, Stuck In a Moment, Kite, Wild Honey (acoustic), Please (acoustic), Bad / 40, Where the Streets Have No Name, I Still Haven't Found What I'm Looking For, PrideBullet the Blue Sky, What's Going On, New York, One, Peace on Earth / Walk On.

That show in Philadelphia ended a nine-day, eight-show road trip for me on the Elevation Tour. That was my longest time following a U2 tour, until my three-month road trip ten years later on the 360 tour when I drove to every U.S. show.

U2 show #42 – December 1, 2001 – Tampa

One month after the Elevation show in Philly and two nights before the U2 show in Tampa, Florida on Saturday December 1, 2001, I had a little pre-U2 concert gathering at my house. My traveling companions for the weekend, Tasha, Jenny and Paola came over my house and we watched U2 videos, concerts and interviews until about one o'clock in the morning. Then with barely three hours sleep, we were off to the airport for the final weekend of the U2 Elevation Tour. It was a bittersweet weekend.

We arrived in sunny, warm Tampa around 11am. Our hotel was absolutely beautiful and it was right next to the Ice Palace, the venue where U2 would play the next night. While walking into our hotel, we noticed Back Street Boy Nick Carter also in the lobby. (This would be significant to me about 13 years later on the Nick and Knight tour, but at the time I had no idea who he was.) Before heading over to the Ice Palace, we had a lovely lunch outside at this beautiful waterfront restaurant.

We were in the GA line by 1:30pm the day before the U2 show, getting numbers 6, 7, 8, and 9. It was a long day in the hot Florida sun. For dinner, we ordered pizza in the GA line, as in they delivered pizza to us outside in the GA line. Around midnight, we got really silly, imagining a lamp post was Darth Vader. You can imagine some pretty crazy things when you are sleep deprived, a bit dehydrated and spending hours and hours on concrete in the GA line waiting to see your 26th U2 Elevation show.

Around 7am the morning, we watched the U2 trucks drive in. Elevation was the sort of low key tour when it took less than 12 hours to assemble the stage. We went back to our hotel to shower and enjoy a nice buffet breakfast. We couldn't try to meet U2 as they drove in because we weren't allowed to leave the GA line once we had our wristbands. They had us locked in those barricades like cattle, and I was very afraid of those barricades ever since I hit my head on one in Pittsburgh. We heard Bono and Edge stopped around 6:30, so I least I didn't miss Larry.

    It became very chaotic when the doors opened with people pushing and running, but somehow we managed to get right up front at the rail between Bono and Adam, even more center than we were for Providence2. Our two days in the GA line had paid off. Paola and I were of course wearing our "Larry Mullen Band" shirts. Garbage opened, and Shirley Manson looked at us and said something like "We have some fans of the Larry Mullen Band here. What else does your shirt say? It's All About Drums. Yes, it is." Shirley was great! We got a chance to talk with her and have our picture taken with her a few months later when Garbage played a show in Philadelphia. Of course we were wearing our "Larry Mullen Band" shirts then also.

    That Elevation show in Tampa was as great as the Baltimore show, the same amazing energy! I was just REALLY into it! U2 played "Angel of Harlem" instead of "Wild Honey," which was great. U2 played all of "Peace on Earth" for the first time. Bono sang "My Sweet Lord" at the end of "Kite" in honor of the passing of George Harrison a few days earlier. It was very touching. The highlight for me of course was when U2 played "Who's Gonna Ride Your Wild Horses" during "Bad!" Just as special was when Larry walked right over to us and gave Paola his drum stick. A much funnier moment was when Bono put on this way too tiny "I Love NY" shirt from a fan. I still don't know how he squeezed into that thing.

The set list for the Elevation show in Tampa on December 1, 2001 was as follows: Elevation, Beautiful Day, Until the End of the World, New Year's Day, I Will Follow, Sunday Bloody Sunday, Stuck In a Moment, Kite / My Sweet Lord, Angel of Harlem, Please (B & E acoustic), Bad / Who's Gonna Ride Your Wild Horses, Where the Streets Have No Name, I Still Haven't Found What I'm Looking For,
Pride, Bullet the Blue Sky, What's Going On, New York, One, Peace on Earth / Walk On.

U2 show #43 – the Last Elevation show - December 2, 2001 – Miami

Immediately following the U2 show in Tampa, we drove to Miami for the Elevation show the next night. Along the way, we stopped at Denny's and seemed like we were there forever. We finally arrived at the American Airlines Arena just before 5am on December 2, 2001, the morning of the final show on the Elevation Tour that had started 10 months prior also in Southern Florida. We got our numbers in the GA line (108, 109, 110 and 111).

We tried to check into our hotel, but apparently our reservation was not guaranteed for a 5am next day arrival at that "fine" establishment. I am much better at planning a U2 tour now. We slept in our car, in the parking lot of the Arena where the GA line was, all four of us (two of us are six feet tall) in a small four-door rental. Somehow we managed a few hours sleep. Around 9am, we checked into our disgusting hotel to shower. It was a far cry from the luxury hotel we stayed at in Tampa the day before. We got our film developed from the Tampa show (remember when had to find a camera store to get our photographs developed?), got lunch and then got back in the GA line.

A while later we went over to this Irish Pub in South Beach to pick up our ETS tickets, along with 12.2.01 Elevation Miami shirts and posters. We went back to the GA line for a bit, got our wristbands and then went over to wait for U2 to arrive. A limo drove in around 4:30pm and supposedly it was Larry, but I couldn't tell who it was. We waited until just about 6pm, but no one else ever drove in. We found out later U2 arrived around 7pm, but did not stop to greet the fans - probably because everyone was already inside.

Once inside the arena, we ended up one person back from the front rail on the far right, Adam's side. Usually I stood right at the rail to have something to lean on and hold on to when I got excited, so this was going to be a new experience for the last Elevation show. I was not very steady to jump in place once "Elevation" started. Garbage again opened the show, but this performance would be very different from the rest and so very exciting for me.

Before Garbage's last song, Shirley Manson said their drummer was fired and he left. All of a sudden, I saw Sammy dart out to the drum kit. Then Larry walked onto the stage in a navy blue shirt. Finally a different shirt from the light blue, grey, maroon shirts he rotated on the tour. I went nuts, literally! Since I didn't have the front rail to hold on to, I put my hand on poor Tasha's shoulder to stabilize myself as I jumped up and down like a pogo stick. I don't think Tasha's shoulder recovered for a day or so. Larry played the drums with Garbage on "Only Happy When it Rains," which will always be my favorite Garbage song. Larry played differently with Garbage. He seemed happier and much more into it and excited, probably because it was a different song that he hasn't played thousands of times. Best opening act ever!

That U2 show in Miami show, the last on the Elevation Tour, was amazing and very emotional! It was the first time I heard "In God's Country," from my favorite *The Joshua Tree*, played live in concert. Bono played the harmonica at the end of it, which just added to magnificence of it. For the first time on that leg of the tour, I heard "Mysterious Ways." U2 again played "Wild Horses" and "My Sweet Lord" like they did the night before in Tampa.

Our friend Matt was pulled up on stage to play "Knockin on Heaven's Door" with U2, and our friend Dan was pulled up again during "Stuck in a Moment." And Tasha finally had her concert moment with Adam when he reached down, squeezed her hand and gave her his guitar pick after "Pride." I had been crying for three songs by this point. I started crying during "Streets," all through my favorite "I Still Haven't Found What I'm Looking For" and into "Pride." It just hit me that this was the last show. Over the past 10 months, I had seen 27 Elevation shows including the first and the last of the tour, plus all the friends I had made and places I had seen. It was a magical tour and a magical night in Miami. After the show, we hung out with everyone outside the arena and just watched the trucks drive away.

The set list for the final Elevation show in Miami on December 2, 2001 was as follows: Elevation, Beautiful Day, Until the End of the World, Mysterious Ways, Out of Control, Sunday Bloody Sunday, Stuck in a Moment, Kite, In God's Country, Knockin' on Heaven's Door, Please (acoustic), Bad / Who's Gonna Ride Your Wild Horses, Where the Streets Have No Name, I Still Haven't Found What I'm Looking For, Pride, Bullet the Blue Sky, What's Going On?, New York, One, My Sweet Lord, Walk On / 40.

Post Elevation Thoughts

The great Elevation Tour was over, and sad doesn't even begin to describe how I felt. It was like a loss. At the time, U2's Elevation Tour was the most amazing experience of my life! I wrote in my journal at the end of 2001, "The two months I spent in Ireland and this Elevation tour were the two best experiences of my life!" The Elevation Tour is still my favorite U2 tour, but the 360 Tour ten years later would probably be the most amazing experience of my life. 2001 was a great year though. From March 24th in Ft. Lauderdale to December 2nd in Miami, I saw 27 fantastic U2 shows, had three wonderful moments with Larry, visited 17 great cities and made many good friends.

My favorite show of the Elevation tour and of any tour was Providence 2, Larry's 40th Birthday on October 31, 2001. Other special shows were Baltimore, the final show in Miami, Jersey1, Boston4, Philly2, and Tampa. The entire Elevation tour was great, but these seven shows were definite stand outs for me. My Larry moments were more than I could have ever hoped for. I've been in love with Larry since I was 14, back in 1987. I never dreamed Larry would hand me his drum stick at the end of the show, hug me before a show, or give me his birthday champagne during a show. Unreal!

For New Year's Eve, I had most of my new U2 friends I had met throughout the year on the Elevation tour over for a U2/New Year's Eve Party. We celebrated our great year of U2 watching U2 videos, discussing the tour and sharing our pictures. Remember this was before Facebook or any social media.

A year later U2 played the Super Bowl halftime show February 3, 2002. I had a little Super Bowl / U2 party at my apartment. It was an amazing performance, and Larry wore a see-through shirt! Tasha and I were screaming as if we were at the U2 show, scaring all our non-U2 fan guests. It would be three more years before I would actually be at another U2 show. Sadly it was never again like it was on the Elevation Tour.

Vertigo

Me watching Larry during "Love and Peace" 2005
(Photo by Jennifer Jamison)

How To Dismantle An Atomic Bomb

On November 22, 2004, U2's *How to Dismantle an Atomic Bomb* was released. Unlike U2's previous offerings, I was not in love with this album no matter how many times I listened to it. But there were a few songs on it that I did love: "Original of the Species," "Sometimes You Can't Make it on Your Own," and "Love and Peace or Else" after hearing it live.

It wasn't until much later I began to appreciate *How to Dismantle an Atomic Bomb*, as it actually is quite a good album. Sadly even with my new appreciation for it, *How to Dismantle an Atomic Bomb* will never be one of my favorite albums because it wasn't my favorite back then. It does not evoke any amazing memories for me and as unintelligent as it may sound, the nostalgia factor has a lot to do with how much I love an album.

Also in November of 2004, the special edition U2 iPod was released. This was my first iPod. It contained 400 songs called *The Complete U2* as well as engraved signatures of Bono, Larry, Edge and Adam on the back. Ten years later it no longer works, but it makes a great piece of U2 memorabilia for my collection.

Even though it had a great, diverse set list including lots of old rarely played U2 songs, I was as disinterested in the Vertigo Tour as I was interested in the Elevation Tour. Before the tour started, I had tickets to 15 shows on Vertigo. As the tour went on, I sold some of my tickets and ended up going to eight concerts on the Vertigo tour. Of those, only three shows were GA.

U2 show #44 – May 14, 2005 – Philadelphia

I left my house in Maryland on May 14, 2005 starting an eight-day road trip consisting of four U2 shows, three Lisa Marie Presley shows, a Broadway show and the Daytime Emmys. This was the second time I went on the road with U2 leaving my house for an extended period of time. The best things really do happen when you don't plan them.

For my first show of the Vertigo tour on May 14, 2005, I was to meet my friend Tasha, my concert buddy from the Elevation Tour, at the Wachovia Center in Philadelphia at 7pm. There was no need to arrive early because we had seats behind the stage, my favorite alternative if I can't get a GA ticket. Our friend Jenny called around 3pm to say she got us GAs. U2 usually released tickets on the day of the show.

Tasha and I went in around 7:30, well after the GA went in. We stood about halfway between the catwalk and soundboard. Kings of Leon opened, and I did not like them at all, and I still don't. During U2's fourth song, "Electric Co.", this lady from U2 came up to us because Tasha was dancing and she said it looked like we were having fun, so she gave us wristbands to get inside the ellipse. On the Vertigo tour, there was a lottery system to see who got into the ellipse, the section closest to the stage, inside the catwalk. It didn't matter if you were the first person in the GA line or the last. It all just depended if your ticket beeped when scanned to see if you got into the ellipse.

Tasha and I went into the ellipse and stood up front one person back from the stage in front of Adam. When Larry sang during "Love and Peace," I ran to the back of the ellipse. I was jumping up and down as if I was on a pogo. U2 played "Running to Stand Still," "An Cat Dubh," "40," "Zoo Station," "Into the Heart," all which they did not play on the Elevation tour. It was a really good show, and I was very excited but I did not feel the same craziness and obsessive need to go to every show as I had on past tours. I was afraid I was losing my love for U2. I wasn't obviously or this book would end here. I just didn't have a great love for the Vertigo tour.

The set list for my first Vertigo show in Philly on May 14, 2005 was as follows: City of Blinding Lights, Vertigo, Elevation, The Electric Co., An Cat Dubh – Into the Heart, Beautiful Day, Miracle Drug, Sometimes You Can't Make It On Your Own, Love and Peace or Else, Sunday Bloody Sunday, Bullet the Blue Sky – When Johnny Comes Marching Home, Running to Stand Still, Pride, Where the Streets Have No Name, One, Zoo Station, The Fly, Mysterious Ways, All Because of You, Yahweh, 40.

On the Road to New Jersey

May 16, 2005

On the morning after the U2 show, I left Philadelphia to drive to Asbury Park, for the Lisa Marie Presley concert on May 16th. It was her last of the tour. I did have GA for her show. It was amazing! I stood up front right at the rail at the stage. Priscilla was there, and Lisa shook my hand and said, "Thank you" at the end of the show. After the show, I drove two hours to my hotel in East Rutherford for the next U2 show on May 17th. I got lost and was exhausted by the time I checked in.

U2 show #45 – May 17, 2005 – East Rutherford

Around 1am my friends Paola and Gina arrived. I woke up at 4am and got a cab into New York City to see Lisa Marie Presley perform on *Good Morning America*. They didn't let us in until after 7am, and Lisa didn't come on until about 8:45. She only sang one song, "Idiot," but it was pretty cool. I was SO close to her and apparently I was on tv because my mom called to say she saw me on tv singing along. Ugh! After *GMA*, I immediately went back to the hotel to rest a bit before the U2 show that night, luckily I had a seat and not GA.

This U2 concert on May 17th Continental Airlines Arena in Jersey was better than the one a few days before in Philadelphia. It was the same set list as in Philly except U2 played "Original of the Species," my favorite off the new *How to Dismantle an Atomic Bomb*, and played "Vertigo" twice, closing the show with it. My seat for this show was great! I was behind the stage, behind Edge about seven rows up. It was very close and a very good view. Kings of Leon opened again, and I still didn't like them. I wrote in my journal that night after the show, "As good as the concert was, I'm just not as into it anymore. I'm considering selling my tickets for the Fall shows and my ticket for the Philly show on Sunday." I actually did sell my ticket for that Philadelphia show, as well as the Fall shows, even my birthday show.

The set list for the first Vertigo show in Jersey on May 17, 2005 was as follows: City of Blinding Lights, Vertigo, Elevation, The Electric Co., An Cat Dubh – Into the Heart, Beautiful Day – Blackbird, Miracle Drug, Sometimes You Can't Make It On Your Own, Love and Peace or Else, Sunday Bloody Sunday, Bullet the Blue Sky – When Johnny Comes Marching Home, Running to Stand Still, Pride, Where the Streets Have No Name, One, Zoo Station, The Fly, Mysterious

Ways, Original of the Species, All Because Of You, Yahweh, 40, Vertigo.

U2 show #46 – May 18, 2005 – East Rutherford

The next night was the second show at Continental Airlines Arena in New Jersey on May 18, 2005, and it was my favorite of the week. Saturday in Philly was great because it was my first one of the tour, and we were on the floor up front in front of Adam. The first show in Jersey the night before had an amazing energy, both from the band and from the audience. U2 played "Original of the Species." This second show in Jersey had the best set list. U2 played "Gloria," "The Ocean," "Bad" and "I Still Haven't Found What I'm Looking For" with a band they pulled out of the audience. I went to the show with Jenny. We had seats on the side of the stage in the last row up top, so we just stood behind our section and had plenty of room to move around and dance. It was just a fun, relaxed time!

The set list for the second Vertigo show in Jersey on May 18, 2005 was as follows: City of Blinding Lights, Vertigo – Stories for Boys – Pump It Up, Elevation, Gloria, The Ocean, Beautiful Day, Miracle Drug, Sometimes You Can't Make It On Your Own, Love and Peace or Else, Sunday Bloody Sunday, Bullet the Blue Sky – When Johnny Comes Marching Home, Running to Stand Still, Pride, Where the Streets Have No Name, One, Zoo Station, The Fly, Mysterious Ways, All Because Of You, Yahweh, I Still Haven't Found What I'm Looking For, Bad – 40

On the Road to New York City

May 19, 2005

On the morning after the U2 show in Jersey, Jenny and I drove into New York City. We went to Lisa Marie Presley's free concert in City Hall Park. I was front row at the rail center stage. It was a great show! After walking around the City for a bit, I went to see *All Shook Up* on Broadway, which was great!

May 20, 2005

The next day, I went back into New York City to go to the Daytime Emmy Awards at Radio City Music Hall. It was so cool! I saw all my favorite stars from *As the World Turns.* Oh how I miss *As the World Turns*!

U2 show #47 – May 21, 2005 – New York City

The next night was the U2 show at Madison Square Garden on May 21st. It was actually my least favorite of the four I saw that week. Kings of Leon opened again – ugh! I saw the show with Tasha, and we had good seats behind the stage not too far up. The only difference in the set list was a David Bowie cover "Jean Genie." U2 played "Original of the Species" again.

At least I got to hear every song U2 played on the Vertigo Tour over the four shows I went to. I wrote in my journal that night after the show, "It's sad, but I'm just not into it anymore. I want to go home. I'm not going to the Philly show tomorrow." Granted I had been on the road for over a week and missing my new puppy, but I was not into the Vertigo tour like I had been on past U2 tours.

The set list for the Vertigo show in NYC on May 21, 2005 was as follows: City of Blinding Lights, Vertigo – Rockaway Beach, Elevation, The Electric Co., An Cat Dubh – Into the Heart, Beautiful Day, Miracle Drug, Sometimes You Can't Make It On Your Own, Love and Peace or Else, Sunday Bloody Sunday, Bullet the Blue Sky – When Johnny Comes Marching Home, Running to Stand Still, Pride, Where the Streets Have No Name, One, Zoo Station, The Fly – The Jean Genie, Mysterious Ways, Original of the Species, All Because Of You, Yahweh, Vertigo.

U2 show #48 – October 19, 2005 – DC

Five months later I went to the two Vertigo shows in Washington, DC at the MCI Center. Because I was not really excited about the Vertigo tour, I sold most of my tickets to the Fall shows, including my birthday show, but I was not going to miss the shows in my hometown where I didn't have to travel. The first of these two shows was on October 19th, the fourth anniversary of the great Elevation show in Baltimore where Larry hugged me. Since U2 were not playing Baltimore, DC was the next best thing.

I went to this show first show in DC with Jennifer. Even though we had GA tickets, we did not wait in the GA line because there was no point with the lottery system. In fact, I worked all day and went into DC after. Luckily for us, Jennifer's ticket beeped when it was scanned, and we were let into the ellipse. As long as one person in your party ticket beeped when scanned, you could get into the ellipse.

We stood in the back of the ellipse next to the catwalk, so when Larry came out during "Love and Peace," I was right in front of him. Larry smiled at me and waved. Of course I was the only six-foot blonde bouncing like a pogo wearing a "Larry Mullen Band" shirt. DC was a great show! My friends Traci and Paola were also there. After the show, about five of us met up and went to the Double T Diner for a little post concert meal.

The set list for the first Vertigo show in DC on October 19, 2005 was as follows: City of Blinding Lights, Vertigo, Elevation, I Will Follow, The Electric Co. – Send in the Clowns, I Still Haven't Found What I'm Looking For – In a Little While, Beautiful Day – Many Rivers to Cross, Miracle Drug, Sometimes You Can't Make It On Your Own, Love and Peace or Else,, Sunday Bloody Sunday, Bullet the Blue Sky, Miss Sarajevo, Pride, Where the Streets Have No Name, One – Ol' Man River, The First Time (acoustic), Stuck In A Moment You Can't Get Out Of, With or Without You, All Because of You, Yahweh, 40.

U2 show #49 – October 20, 2005 – DC

The next morning on October 20th, I woke up and did it all over again. I didn't have to work on the day of that second Vertigo show in DC. That show turned out to be my favorite of the tour. U2 played four out of my top five favorite songs – "I Still Haven't Found What I'm Looking For," "Bad," "Pride" and "Who's Gonna Ride Your Wild Horses." And even more special was I saw this show with my friends Jennifer, Paola and Gina. It was great to be able to see it with everyone. We were again inside the ellipse (thanks to Jennifer's ticket scanning) standing right where Larry shouted out "RELEASE!" during "Love and Peace," and that night I got the subtle Larry nod.

The set list for the second Vertigo show in DC on October 20, 2005 was as follows: City of Blinding Lights, Vertigo, Elevation, The Electric Co., Out of Control, I Still Haven't Found What I'm Looking For, Beautiful Day – Many Rivers to Cross, Miracle Drug, Sometimes You Can't Make It On Your Own, Love and Peace or Else, Sunday Bloody Sunday, Bullet the Blue Sky, Happy Birthday, Miss Sarajevo, Pride, Where the Streets Have No Name, One, Walk On (acoustic), Who's Gonna Ride Your Wild Horses, With or Without You, All Because of You, Bad.

U2 show #50 – November 4, 2005 – Las Vegas

My last shows on the Vertigo Tour were at the MGM Grand in Las Vegas, Nevada. Any excuse to go to Vegas, right? I may not have been that into the Vertigo Tour, but I am always into Vegas! My best friend, Cindy, went with me. She's not necessarily a U2 fan, although she has been to a few shows with me, but she's always up for a trip to Vegas. We arrived in Las Vegas the morning of the first U2 show on November 4, 2005, coincidently the 17th anniversary of *Rattle and Hum* the movie.

Since I had seats and not GA, we took our time. We checked into Bally's, where I always stay in Vegas, and then had pizza at New York New York, who has phenomenal pizza by the way. We walked over to MGM to check out the GA line situation, even though I had a seat for the show. We gambled at Boardwalk Casino, shopped at the Venetian and Alladin and then had dinner at Café Lux, one of our favorites in Vegas.

I walked up to the MGM Grand Arena and took my seat behind the stage. It is where I like to sit when I don't have GA, so I can see Larry, plus it is really close to the stage. Damien Marley opened, but he was not very exciting even though he is Bob Marley's son. There was an Elvis impersonator on the floor section, so during "Love and Peace or Else," Bono tried to sing it like Elvis. Bono sang "Can't Help Falling in Love" after "One." U2 played one of my all-time favorites "Who's Gonna Ride Your Wild Horses!" It was a really good show. Not bad for my 50th U2 show. I was up for over 22 hours, it was a very long, but a very good day.

The set list for the first Vertigo show in Vegas on November 4, 2005 was as follows: City of Blinding Lights, Vertigo, Elevation, The Electric Co. – Send in the Clowns, The Ocean, I Still Haven't Found What I'm Looking For – In a Little While, Beautiful Day, Miracle Drug, Sometimes You Can't Make It On Your Own, Stuck In a Moment You Can't Get Out Of, Love and Peace or Else, Sunday Bloody Sunday, Bullet the Blue Sky, Miss Sarajevo, Pride, Where the Streets Have No Name, One – Can't Help Falling In Love, Walk On (acoustic), Who's Gonna Ride Your Wild Horses, With or Without You, All Because of You, Yahweh, 40.

U2 show #51 – November 5, 2005 – Las Vegas, NV

After being up for over 22 hours, I should have slept all day but it was Vegas, so after only four hours sleep I was up and back at the slots. Cindy and I were having a blast in Lost Wages, uh I mean Las Vegas. We played the slots all day on Freemont Street, at Hard Rock, Treasure Island, the Mirage, the Flamingo and Paris before going to the U2 show that night on November, 5, 2005.

I walked down to the MGM Grand Arena after our dinner at Paris, leaving Cindy playing the slots. I again sat in the seats behind the stage as I had the previous night. This second Vegas show was amazing! Mary J Blige sang on "One," and Brandon Flowers, the lead singer of the Killers, sang on "In a Little While." Unlike the previous night, U2 played "Zoo Station," "The Fly," "Until the End of the World" and "Mysterious Ways." After the show, I walked back to Paris and found Cindy sitting at that same slot machine she was at when I left her a few hours earlier.

The set list for my last Vertigo show in Las Vegas on November 5, 2005 was as follows: City of Blinding Lights, Vertigo, Elevation, Mysterious Ways, Until the End of the World, I Still Haven't Found What I'm Looking For, Beautiful Day – All These Things That I've Done, Miracle Drug, Sometimes You Can't Make It On Your Own, Love and Peace or Else, Sunday Bloody Sunday, Bullet the Blue Sky, Miss Sarajevo, Pride, Where the Streets Have No Name, One, Zoo Station, The Fly, With or Without You, Happy Birthday, All Because of You, In a Little While, Bad.

Post Vertigo Thoughts

The U2 Vertigo Tour had come to an end, and I wasn't sad as I had been after previous tours. Vertigo had a great set list, but I just wasn't into it. I am not sure if I was so disinterested in the Vertigo Tour because of my lack of enthusiasm for *How to Dismantle an Atomic Bomb*, or because of the lack of GA line experience resulting in less of a community feeling, or because I was very into Lisa Marie Presley who was headlining her own tour for the first time, or because I had just bought a house, adopted a puppy and had a real 9-5 job for the first time in my life. Or was it just because Larry had really bad hair on the Vertigo tour? Whatever the case, I did make it to eight Vertigo shows and will never forget that great moment in each show when Larry would walk out on the catwalk and duet with Bono during "Love and Peace or Else." Right in front of me, Larry would stand beating that drum shouting "Release! Release! Release!"

After the Vertigo tour, I was scared I had lost my love for U2. To lose a passion like that would be devastating. I feel sorry for people who don't know that sheer joy. But not to fear, my passion for U2 returned a few years later, and quite possibly greater than ever.

U23D 2008

Three years after the Vertigo Tour, U2 released a concert movie in 3D that was playing in theaters across America. On January 23, 2008, Tasha and I went to the first showing of *U23D* in Baltimore at the Imax Theatre. It was amazing! It was just like being at the U2 show. Tasha and I were screaming as if we were actually at the concert. It is ironic because I wasn't that excited during the Vertigo tour, but I was VERY excited watching *U23D*, which was recorded from the Vertigo tour. This was proof (and comfort) that my passion for U2 was alive and well. I guess I just took 2005 off from it. I went on to see *U23D* three more times, and even got my Dad to go with me. It would be another year and a half before I would actually see U2 in concert.

360 (2009)

Larry singing "Unknown Caller" Oklahoma 2009
(Photo by Deena Dietrich)

No Line on the Horizon

No Line on the Horizon was released on February 27, 2009, just seven months after I moved to Memphis, Tennessee. I immediately fell in love with U2's new album just as I had with *All That You Can't Leave Behind*. My favorite songs off of *No Line* were and still are "Get on Your Boots," "I'll Go Crazy if I Don't Go Crazy Tonight," "Breathe," "No Line on the Horizon," and "Moment of Surrender." A lot of people don't care too much for *No Line on the Horizon*, but I love it. I got *No Line* the day it came out and listened to it nonstop, literally I listened to nothing else. It seemed my U2 obsession had returned after a brief vacation during Vertigo, and I was so relieved it had.

U2 promoted their new release with five consecutive nights on *Late Night with David Letterman* and a mini concert and interview at Fordham University broadcasted on *Good Morning America*. Shortly after the release of *No Line on the Horizon*, U2 announced they would go on the road that Fall and the following Summer playing stadiums again on the 360 tour. My initial plan was to go to the U2 shows in Chicago, Raleigh, Atlanta and Oklahoma. I had never been to Chicago or Atlanta. The U2 show in Raleigh was the day before my birthday and the show in Oklahoma was on Tasha's birthday. I booked hotels in those cities even before tickets went on sale. By July, I had added two more cities on my 360 tour. I decided to take a trip back east to visit my family and friends and see the U2 shows in Washington, DC and Charlottesville, Virginia along the way.

U2 show #52 – 360 Opening Night in North America - September 12, 2009 – Chicago

On September 11, 2009 the day before the opening of 360 in North America, my friend David and I drove eight hours from Memphis to Chicago. We left Memphis at 6am and were in Chicago by 2pm. It was my first time in Chicago, and I was so excited! Before even checking into our hotel, we went straight to Soldier Field to check out the GA line situation. There were folks hanging out on the grassy knoll across from the parking lot. We got our wristbands numbers 115 and 116. We couldn't get onto the stadium lot until 6am the next day, so we went to check into the Travelodge hotel across from Grant Park and got settled.

That night, David and I walked down the street to Buddy Guy's Blues Club for a beer. It was a very cool, laid back place with no cover and a nice staff. As we were leaving, Buddy Guy walks in! I freaked out and froze. Buddy stopped at the souvenir counter where I was going to buy a tee shirt. David asked him for a picture, but Buddy kind of brushed him off saying to come back later. We left with no picture with Buddy, but it was still pretty cool. We took a walk down Michigan Avenue past Grant Park before going back to our hotel. Tasha arrived a little later.

The next morning on September 12, 2009 the day of the first U2 360 show in North America, we woke up at 5am and in the GA line at Soldier Field by 6am. It was a long, hot day. Windy city my ass! Chicago was hot! We sat in the sun in the GA line all day! But we had fun and even met up with some of our old friends from the Elevation tour. It wasn't the most organized GA line in U2 history. It was a bit crowded and sort of pushy, but not too bad. This would be my last time spending all day, 12 hours, waiting in a U2 GA line.

Finally out of the sun, we got in this little holding area where there was lots of pushing. We got our GA floor wristbands then everyone started running. My wristband fell off, so I had to quickly grab it while Tasha was yelling at me. But luckily we were able to get inside the inner circle. Since we couldn't be up front at the rail, we decided to stand at the back of the circle in the center along the catwalk. I had no idea what to expect since I had not been following the first leg of the tour in Europe. Snow Patrol opened. I am not a huge fan, contrary to most U2 fans, but I like one song they do.

The lights went down and out walked Larry Mullen Jr., by himself. I could barely contain my excitement. There was Tasha standing next to me again like at the final Elevation show in Miami when Larry played with Garbage. I again used her shoulder to stabilize myself as I jumped up and down. I really need to make sure I am always standing at a railing so I have something to hold on to. Larry started playing the drums, a little drum solo that emerged into "Breathe." Then the rest of the band came out. Of course Bono came out last making the grand entrance. The Larry excitement didn't stop there. Larry sang on "Get on Your Boots," "Unknown Caller," and "Moment of Surrender." And he walked around playing his conga during "I'll Go Crazy if I Don't Go Crazy Tonight." I was of course wearing my 'Larry Mullen Band' shirt, but he didn't stop in front of us.

It was at this first 360 show in the U.S. when I heard "Unforgettable Fire" for the first time! That song has always been one of my favorites. Also for the first time, I heard "MLK." U2 played "I Still Haven't Found What I'm Looking For," "Pride" and "Bad" for the only time that leg of the tour. I loved that show! I was very emotional. I cried. I was so excited and so drained after. Just like the good old days of Elevation. I was elated to realize my passion for U2 had indeed returned after taking a break on the Vertigo tour.

The set list for Opening Night of the 360 tour in North America on September 12, 2009 in Chicago was as follows: Breathe, No Line On The Horizon, Get On Your Boots, Magnificent, Beautiful Day - Far Far Away - Blackbird, Elevation, I Still Haven't Found What I'm Looking For - Stand By Me, Stuck In A Moment, Unknown Caller, The Unforgettable Fire, City of Blinding Lights, Vertigo, I'll Go Crazy If I Don't Go Crazy Tonight (remix), Sunday Bloody Sunday - Oliver's Army, Pride, MLK, Walk On - You'll Never Walk Alone, Where the Streets Have No Name, One, Bad - Fool To Cry - 40, Ultraviolet, With or Without You, Moment of Surrender.

U2 show #53 – September 13, 2009 – Chicago

The next day in Chicago was much more relaxed. We stayed in our hotel room until noon, then Tasha and I went to Wrigley Field for the Cubs game. We took a cab to and from the game, so I got to see a little bit more of the city. Wrigley Field was the main reason I had always wanted to visit Chicago – and it didn't disappoint. I loved Wrigley Field and the surrounding area! We only stayed for four innings, but we walked all the way around the outside of Wrigley, bought souvenirs and took in the whole Wrigley experience. (I would go back to Wrigley the next year and stay for the whole game.) We got back to the hotel and took a little nap before heading to Soldier Field for the second U2 360 show.

We did not wait in the GA line for the second 360 show in Chicago on September 13th. We went in after the GA line, around 6pm, and got a closer spot to the stage than we did the night before – plus it was much less crowded. We were inside the inner circle on the side, Adam's side. My old U2 friend Mike stood with us, which made the show even better. It was great to see a U2 show with him again, just like the good old days of ZooTV. U2 played "Your Blue Room" for the first time ever. Not a favorite of mine, but it was cool to be at the debut. Other changes to the set list from the first night were U2 played "Stay" and "Until the End of the World," but did not play "Pride," "Bad" or "Stuck in a Moment." In fact, this was the first time "Pride" was not played at a U2 show since the middle of the Elevation Tour. This second 360 show was more relaxed and fun, but the first one was intense and exciting because it was the first one and it had a better set list.

      The set list for the second 360 show in North America in Chicago on September 13, 2009 was as follows: Breathe, No Line On The Horizon, Get On Your Boots - Blue Suede Shoes, Magnificent, Beautiful Day - Far Far Away - King Of Pain, I Still Haven't Found What I'm Looking For, Elevation, Your Blue Room, Unknown Caller, Until the End of the World, Stay (Faraway, So Close), The Unforgettable Fire, City of Blinding Lights, Vertigo, I'll Go Crazy If I Don't Go Crazy Tonight (remix) - I Want To Take You Higher - Don't Stop Til You Get Enough, Sunday Bloody Sunday - Rock The Casbah, MLK, Walk On, One, Amazing Grace, Where the Streets Have No Name - All You Need Is Love, Ultraviolet, With or Without You, Moment of Surrender.

On the Road to DC

September 26, 2009
      I left my house in Memphis on a twelve-day road trip to see four U2 360 shows. This was the longest time I had ever been on the road with U2, until the last leg of the tour. I took my dogs Elvis and Cilla to the vet to board them while I was

gone. I can't believe I left them for 12 days. I did not make that mistake again. I would take them with me on the last leg of the tour.

I had three days before the U2 show in DC on September 29th. The first day was the worst. I made it from Memphis, Tennessee to Wytheville, Virginia in just over eight and a half hours driving 568 miles in the pouring rain and fog. It was 77 degrees when I left Memphis, and was 55 degrees when I got to Wytheville, and I was wearing shorts! The things we endure for those Irish lads.

September 27, 2009

The next day was great. I left Wytheville at 7:45am and got to my best friend Cindy's house before 12:30pm. I got to hang out with her girls, eat Ledo's pizza (which I missed so much living in Memphis), watch football and celebrate my birthday a week early. Just after 5pm, I finally made it to my parents' house. We went out to Jilly's, so I could watch the Broncos game.

September 28, 2009

The next day my Mom, Cindy, Kathy (Cindy's mom) and I went to Charlestown Casino and had a great time playing the slots. That night I felt as if I might be getting sick, which was unfortunate since I was about to embark on four U2 shows in seven days. It was going to be intense!

U2 show #54 – September 29, 2009 – DC

So of course when I should have slept to rest up for the next week, I woke up at 5am the morning of the U2 show in DC on September 29th. I left the house at 2pm, was parked at

FedEx Field by 3, said Hi to my friends in the GA line, got my Red Zone ticket from a U2 friend I had met online, and was in the Red Zone line by 3:30. This was my first time with a Red Zone ticket, a higher priced GA ticket benefitting (RED) and the Global Fund to fight AIDS in Africa. I was about 10th in line. The Red Zone ticket line was much smaller than the GA line. Kelly, a U2 friend from high school and back in the ZooTV days, stood with me and we caught up.

They split the line into boys and girls to search us. They let us in around 5:15 when everyone else went in, but no one told us where to go. We weren't at field level. It took forever to get down to the field. When I finally did reach the Red Zone, I saw that it was a part of the GA sectioned off on either side of the stage on the outside of the catwalk. Instead of going into the designated Red Zone, I went inside the inner circle and stood up front at the rail in front of Adam. This was my first time standing at the front rail at the stage since the Elevation Tour. It was good to be back!

Muse opened and then U2 took the stage. Of course Larry came out first, so there was screaming. U2 did not play "No Line on the Horizon" or "Unknown Caller" and still no "Bad" or "Pride." During "City of Blinding Lights," Bono brought up a kid on the catwalk and ran around with him then gave him his glasses. Apparently, Bono would do this at most other shows, but at the time I thought it was unique. During "Sunday Bloody Sunday" Bono pulled Amp (a friend of a friend) up on stage who was standing not too far from me holding an American flag. They sang and hugged. During "Mysterious Ways," Bono instructed, "Shake your big fat asses!" During "I'll Go Crazy if I Don't Go Crazy Tonight," Bono shouted, "Larry Mullen goes crazy! Larry Mullen is crazy!" He's so clever. Haha. There were many politicians at the show as I saw lots of extra security. Bono introduced the members of the band as politicians.

My favorite part of the show was when Larry saw my "Larry Mullen Band" shirt and smiled and nodded. I was taking a picture of Adam for Tasha with the bright light behind him so he looked almost angelic. The bright light was on Adam and I was right in front of Adam so the light was on me. Larry's drum kit started to turn around to face behind the stage during "Beautiful Day." And as Larry was turning, I started jumping and screaming and that's when he saw me. A girl two people down came up to me after the concert and said, "I saw Larry smile at you." AAAHHHH!!!!

That 360 show in DC was a great show! I really enjoyed standing up front at the rail like I had for all those Elevation shows. That was the closest, most centered spot I stood at any show of the 360 tour. Even though it didn't have the best set list, there was a great energy from the band and the audience.

The set list for the 360 show in DC on September 29, 2009 was as follows: Breathe, Magnificent, Get On Your Boots, Mysterious Ways, I Still Haven't Found What I'm Looking For - Stand By Me, Elevation, Your Blue Room, Beautiful Day - Blackbird, New Year's Day, Stuck In A Moment, The Unforgettable Fire, City of Blinding Lights, Vertigo, I'll Go Crazy If I Don't Go Crazy Tonight (remix) - Let's Dance - Don't Stop Til You Get Enough, Sunday Bloody Sunday, MLK, Walk On, One, Amazing Grace, Where the Streets Have No Name, Ultraviolet, With or Without You, Moment of Surrender.

U2 show #55 – October 1, 2009 – Charlottesville

After the U2 show in DC, I went back to my parents' house and spent the night and the next day there. I left around

11:15am the morning of the 360 show in Charlottesville, Virginia on October 1, 2009. I arrived at our hotel around 2:30pm. That day was a comedy of errors, actually an annoyance of traffic. I have never been fond of Virgina, and that day in Charlottesville did not change my mind one bit. I had to wait in line for an hour to check into our crappy Super8 motel. Tasha and her sister met me at the hotel. We left around 4:15pm for the concert and didn't find our parking lot (I had purchased parking ahead of time) at Scott Stadium at the University of Virginia until almost 6pm. It took us almost two hours to drive a few miles. I hate Virginia traffic!

    Of course we could walk right in when we got there because the GA line had already went in. We stood inside the circle side stage – Adam side on the rail, but literally on the side. I was starting to learn you didn't have to wait all day in line to get a good spot close to the stage – as long as you didn't mind not being front and center. I liked being up front on the side of the stage because there was more room. And it worked out well for us that night in Charlottesville because Bono sang the first verse of "Unforgettable Fire" to us on his way to the bridge connecting to the catwalk.

    Another great moment of the show was during "Get on Your Boots," which was quickly becoming one of my favorite songs of the 360 show. I'm not sure if it was because we were standing directly to the side of the stage or the vocals were turned up too loud, but I could clearly hear Larry screaming the "Hey Hey Hey"'s during "Boots." I never heard it that clearly again for the rest of the tour. Because we had so much room and didn't have to stay in our 'spot,' I was able to follow Larry to the back during "I'll Go Crazy." A tactic I would perfect as the 360 tour went on. We also went back behind the stage during "Moment of Surrender" to watch U2 leave, but unfortunately they left on the other side. After the show, it only took us five minutes to get back to our hotel (as opposed to the two hours it took us to get there!)

During the 360 tour, I always said the Charlottesville show was my least favorite of the tour, but that was more because of the terrible traffic and how long it took us to get there. But listening to the bootleg after, it really was a good show. U2 put "No Line on the Horizon" back in the set list, and Bono talked about the history of Thomas Jefferson's hometown. It was also the first time U2 had ever played Charlottesville, so that was special. And my good friends Abbey, Jennifer and Mike were also there. It is funny how circumstances of a concert, rather than the concert itself, can taint your experience. It's not always all about the music, but it is always all about the drums.

The set list for the 360 show in Charlottesville on October 1, 2009 was as follows: Breathe, Get On Your Boots, Mysterious Ways, Beautiful Day - The Hands That Built America, No Line On The Horizon, Magnificent, Elevation, Your Blue Room, New Year's Day, I Still Haven't Found What I'm Looking For - Movin' On Up, Stuck In A Moment, The Unforgettable Fire, City of Blinding Lights, Vertigo, I'll Go Crazy If I Don't Go Crazy Tonight (remix) - Thank You - I Want To Take You Higher, Sunday Bloody Sunday - People Get Ready, MLK, Walk On - You'll Never Walk Alone, One, Amazing Grace, Where the Streets Have No Name, Ultraviolet, With or Without You, Moment of Surrender.

U2 show #56 – October 3, 2009 – Raleigh, NC (my "birthday" show)

The morning after the U2 show in Charlottesville on October 2, 2009, I left for Raleigh, NC – and I couldn't have been happier to get out of Virginia! I stayed with Vicki, one of my best friends. I was exhausted that night so we just stayed in and got Quizno's for dinner and watched tv. The day of the U2 show on October 3, 2009, we went out to breakfast and lunch and watched college football until Tasha and her other sister (a different sister from the one who went to the Charlottesville show with us) came over.

  Around 4pm, we left for the show. Luckily Vicki only lived about 15 minutes or so from Carter-Finley Stadium at North Carolina State University. As we were getting out of the car, we heard screams. We ran toward them, but we were too late. We had missed Bono by mere seconds. He had stopped to greet the fans waiting and sign autographs. Luckily Larry and Adam did not stop, so Tasha and I were ok. And even better, we actually made it to the concert. Apparently, there was so much traffic people were abandoning their cars on the road so they wouldn't miss the show. If U2 are going to play colleges, there really needs to be a better way in and out. These colleges cannot handle 80,000 U2 fans driving to the stadium at the same time.

  After our near miss with Bono, we walked toward the GA line but were distracted by the sound check. We stood and listened. I was SO excited U2 was rehearsing "In a Little While," my favorite song from *All That You Can't Leave Behind*. I was also excited at the song U2 was rehearsing which I affectionately dubbed 'Big Deena' as I thought it was in honor of my birthday. That song was actually David Bowie's "The Jean Genie." I swear it sounded like Bono was singing, "Big Deena!"

  After the GA line went in, we followed. We went into the inner circle and stood at the back rail on Adam's side at the catwalk. Muse opened again. This was the third time I had seen Muse open for U2 and they were starting to grow on me. I loved that they had two drummers! It was a great birthday show for me, a day early. There was a full moon, it was big and beautiful! Bono even mentioned it. Many of my friends from the Elevation Tour were there as well as my old U2 friend Mike. It was pretty much the same set list as the Charlottesville show except instead of "Your Blue Room," U2 played "In a Little While!" I was SO excited. Not too much of a surprise since I had heard it during the sound check, but that is always not a guarantee. I had not heard "In A Little While" since the Elevation tour eight years prior, and that night in Raleigh I heard it twice.

We again went behind the stage during "Moment of Surrender" to watch U2 leave, but again they exited on the other side of the stage. We got to the parking lot and it was a stand still. At midnight I shouted out to everyone that it was my birthday! Curiously, no one cared. The next day, on my actual birthday October 4th, at Vicki's we watched football, ate pizza and played with dogs. Pretty much a perfect birthday! A great birthday!

The set list for my almost-birthday 360 show in Raleigh on October 3, 2009 was as follows: Breathe, Get On Your Boots, Mysterious Ways, Beautiful Day - C Moon, No Line On The Horizon, Magnificent, Elevation, In A Little While, New Year's Day, I Still Haven't Found What I'm Looking For - Stand By Me, Stuck In A Moment, The Unforgettable Fire, City of Blinding Lights, Vertigo, I'll Go Crazy If I Don't Go Crazy Tonight (remix) - Thank You, Sunday Bloody Sunday - Rock The Casbah - People Get Ready, MLK, Walk On - You'll Never Walk Alone, One, Amazing Grace, Where the Streets Have No Name, Ultraviolet, With or Without You, Moment of Surrender.

On the Road to Atlanta

October 5, 2009

The day after my birthday I left Vicki's apartment around 6:30am and was in Atlanta by 1pm. When I got out of the car, I could barely walk because my knees were so stiff and sore. The GA life is a rough life. It was my first time in Atlanta, and I had booked a hotel right downtown close to everything I wanted to see. My room had a refrigerator and microwave, which is very important on road trips as I pack a cooler with sandwiches, drinks and snacks to keep the cost as low as possible.

Even though I wasn't feeling well (I knew back in Maryland I was getting sick), I went to Martin Luther King Jr's birthplace, gravesite and Ebenezer Church. These are the MLK sites I had been wanted to see for a while. I went to The Varsity, which is the largest Drive-In in the U.S., but I didn't eat because I was feeling worse. I came back to the hotel, drank cranberry juice, took ibuprofen and laid down for a while. I fell asleep around 7pm.

U2 show #57 – October 6, 2009 – Atlanta

After 14 hours in bed, I finally got up at 9am on the morning of the U2 360 show in Atlanta on October 6th. I still didn't feel well, but headed to the Georgia Dome and was in the GA line just before noon. I was probably about 350-400 people back. I was so sick I actually fell asleep sitting in my chair in the GA line in the middle of the day. It was a very organized GA line. They let about 50 to 100 people in at a time, but then there were a few gates and you had to walk around to get down to the floor. Somehow even though I was

300 to 400 people back in line, I got a spot at the front rail in front of Adam, about 3 people to the right of where I was in DC with my Red Zone ticket. Further proof there is no need to wait in line overnight or all day for 12 hours. That was the last time I actually waited in the GA line, and it was also the last time I stood at the front rail.

Muse again opened. U2's vocals were loud like Charlottesville, so I could really hear Larry's "Hey Hey Hey" during "Get on Your Boots" again. Even though we were in Atlanta, home of Martin Luther King, and I was wearing my 'U2 MLK Pride' shirt, U2 still did not play "Pride." They hadn't played it since the first show in Chicago, but I thought for sure U2 would play "Pride" in Atlanta. At least they played "MLK" – not the same though. I was so sick during the show, literally hanging onto the front rail, that I left during "One." First time I have ever left a U2 show early, but I was so sick I just couldn't make it. Thank goodness there weren't any changes to the set list after I left.

The set list from the 360 show in Atlanta on October 6, 2009 was as follows: Breathe, Get On Your Boots, Mysterious Ways, Beautiful Day - Blackbird, I Still Haven't Found What I'm Looking For - Stand By Me, Stuck In A Moment, No Line On The Horizon, Magnificent, Elevation, Until the End of the World, The Unforgettable Fire, City of Blinding Lights, Vertigo, I'll Go Crazy If I Don't Go Crazy Tonight (remix) Thank You, Sunday Bloody Sunday - People Get Ready, MLK, Walk On - You'll Never Walk Alone, One, Amazing Grace, Where the Streets Have No Name - All You Need Is Love, Ultraviolet, With or Without You, Moment of Surrender.

On the Road to Oklahoma

October 16, 2009

    Almost two weeks after the U2 show in Atlanta, Tasha and I were off for the show in Oklahoma on October 18, 2009. This time it was Tasha's birthday, her actual birthday. Two nights before the show, Tasha flew into Memphis where I was living at the time. That night we drove just over four hours and spent the night in Ft. Smith, Arkansas. We had to make a pit stop in Stillwater on the way to the U2 show in Norman.

October 17, 2009

    The next morning we left Ft. Smith just before 9am and arrived at Oklahoma State University in Stillwater around 11:30am. We circled the campus a few times and then had lunch at Panera before walking over to the Parade. We were there for the OSU Sea of Orange Homecoming Parade because Tasha's favorite Robin Ventura was the Grand Marshall of the parade along with Barry Sanders and Garth Brooks. The three were also getting inducted into the OSU Hall of Fame. We waited at the start of the parade until Robin, Barry and Garth got into their cars. Then we walked, sometimes ran, along side them following the parade.

    After the parade, we followed some girl to the stadium where we discovered Robin, Garth, Barry were inside doing a press conference. They came out and we got to meet them. Robin came out first. I asked him "Will you please take a picture with her (tasha)? Her birthday is tomorrow." He said, "Yes" and put his arm around her tightly and said, "Happy Birthday early." I got the picture then they quickly dispersed, so I only got one. We didn't actually speak to Garth Brooks or Barry Sanders, but we got pictures of them. It was one of those once in a lifetime events we were able to attend because everything came together just right – Robin Ventura in a homecoming parade the day before the U2 show less than two hours away.

Late that afternoon, we headed for Norman, Oklahoma. We went to Oklahoma Memorial Stadium at the University of Oklahoma where the U2 show was going to be the following night. We wanted to see the stage, but all we could see was the claw sticking out and couldn't tell if it was in the middle of the field or in one of the end zones. We checked into our hotel at the Riverwind Casino, had a yummy dinner at the buffet, then played the slots. Whenever I have a chance add casinos to my trips, I take it.

U2 show #58 – October 18, 2009 – Norman

The next morning on October 18, 2009, Tasha's birthday and the U2 show, we relaxed in the casino. We enjoyed our free breakfast buffet at the casino and played the slots for a couple of hours. Actually I played while Tasha watched. Then we got a pizza and went back to our room to watch football. Have to conserve energy while on tour. We left for the show around 2:15. There was no traffic and very easy parking. We waited for U2 to arrive. This was to be my pattern for the rest of the tour – arriving at the venue by 3pm to wait for U2 to arrive with hopes of meeting them. U2 arrived a little after 5pm but didn't stop. Bono rolled down his window and waved, but no one else did.

We went into the stadium after the GA line. The stage was in the middle of the field, which is actually 360 – finally! Not only was the stage in the middle of the field, but it faced the sidelines, instead of the end zone. It was the smallest GA I have ever seen. The inner circle took up almost all of the GA section. The people in the front row of the seats, which were bleachers, were almost at the catwalk. It was crazy! We ended up standing somewhere in the middle of the inner circle, not at the front rail and not at the rail at the catwalk. We were of course more towards Adam's side for Tasha – it was her birthday.

This show in Oklahoma was a great one! Much like the DC show, it had the same relaxed, happy vibe. Black Eyed Peas opened. I am not a huge fan of theirs, but they were a much better opening act than Snow Patrol or Muse. They just really got the crowd into it, and it's an opening act's job to hype the crowd. For me, the highlight of this show was during "I'll Go Crazy if I Don't Go Crazy Tonight." Usually my highlights were during "Boots" or "I'll Go Crazy." I went behind the stage where Larry was going to be with his conga. Wearing my "Larry Mullen Band" shirt and jumping up and down yelling "Larry!" and being the only one back there, Larry saw me, waved and nodded! Of course I went behind the stage both times Larry's drum kit rotated and faced the back during "Beautiful Day" and "Sunday Bloody Sunday." Everyone else at the show is facing front watching Bono, and I'm running behind the stage to watch Larry. I was happy to see "In a Little While" remained in the set list and for the return of "Unknown Caller," which I hadn't heard since Chicago.

The set list for Tasha's birthday show in Norman on October 18, 2009 was as follows: Breathe, Get On Your Boots, Magnificent, Mysterious Ways, Beautiful Day - God Only Knows, I Still Haven't Found What I'm Looking For - Stand By Me, Stuck In A Moment, No Line On The Horizon, Elevation, In A Little While, Unknown Caller, Until the End of the World, The Unforgettable Fire, City of Blinding Lights, Vertigo, I'll Go Crazy If I Don't Go Crazy Tonight (remix) - Thank You - Don't Stop Til You Get Enough, Sunday Bloody Sunday, MLK, Walk On - You'll Never Walk Alone, One,

Amazing Grace, Where the Streets Have No Name, Ultraviolet, With or Without You, Moment of Surrender.

U2 show #59 – October 23, 2009 – Las Vegas

A few days later on October 23, 2009, the day of the U2 show, I flew to Las Vegas. I had to wait in line for an hour to get my rental car. I've never rented a car in Vegas before, but Tasha was staying for free (through her work) at the Red Rocks casino outside of town. Plus it was a hotel and casino called Red Rocks! I got to the hotel, Tasha and I had lunch at the casino buffet, then we drove to Sam Boyd Stadium at the University of Las Vegas. We were there by 3pm and met up with our old Elevation friends Ruth, Melissa and Matt, Ayaz, and Otto. Bono stopped and signed autographs and talked with everyone waiting. Unfortunately, we were stuck behind the fence, so we just got pictures.

That Vegas show was my favorite of that leg of the 360 tour. It was so relaxing and had a great energy. We stood on the side of the stage (Adam's side of course) at the rail, similar to where we were in Charlottesville. Black Eyed Peas opened again, but they weren't as good as they were in Oklahoma. But Fergie did interact with us a lot, so that was fun. Bill Clinton was at the show, as was Larry's dad, but we didn't see either of them.

The set list was the same as in Oklahoma, except Bono sang Elvis' "Viva Las Vegas" after my favorite "I Still Haven't Found What I'm Looking For" / "Stand By Me," so I was obviously freaking out. And if that wasn't enough during the band introductions, Bono called Larry the "Elvis of the band." The vocals were really loud, so I could really hear Larry's "Hey Hey Hey"'s during "Get on Your Boots" again. I left the front rail at the end of "Vertigo" so I could see Larry start "I'll Go Crazy." I was back there alone again wearing my "Larry Mullen Band" shirt but I wasn't jumping and screaming this time, but he still saw me, smiled and waved. I stayed and watched the rest of the show from behind the stage. Larry was facing me during "Sunday Bloody Sunday." Then Bono came back and was singing to me. We waited for U2 outside after the show, but they did not stop. In fact we never saw them, so either they left early or really late. We went back to Red Rocks and ate at Fat Burger, whose veggie burger is quite filling by the way.

The set list for the 360 show in Vegas on October 23, 2009 was as follows: Breathe, Get on Your Boots, Magnificent, Mysterious Ways, Beautiful Day / In God's Country / Fix You, I Still Haven't Found What I'm Looking For / Stand By Me / Viva Las Vegas, Stuck in a Moment, No Line on the Horizon, Elevation, In a Little While, Unknown Caller, Until the End of the World, Unforgettable Fire, City of Blinding Lights, Vertigo / All These Things I've Done, I'll Go Crazy If I Don't Go Crazy Tonight, Sunday Bloody Sunday, MLK, Walk On / You'll Never Walk Alone, One / Amazing Grace, Where the Streets Have No Name, Ultra Violet, With or Without You, Moment of Surrender.

October 24, 2009

The next morning we woke up early for some reason. We went to Freemont Street and tried to recreate the video for "I Still Haven't Found What I'm Looking For." There was some sort of car show / street festival. I saw Elvis Presley's good friend Joe Espisito sitting on the sidewalk at a table. He was selling his book Elvis *Intimate and Rare* and signing autographs. I was so excited to meet him because he is one of Elvis' friends I had yet to meet. Ironically, I was wearing an Elvis shirt. Joe said he liked it. I bought his book and he autographed it. I told Joe I lived in Memphis and asked if he was going to be there for birthday week, but he said he was going to be in Vegas for the opening of Viva Elvis Cirque de Soleil show, which I saw the following year. We went back to Red Rocks and had a fantastic Italian dinner with Tasha's coworkers and then played the slots for a few more hours.

October 25, 2009

The next day I was exhausted and was kind of happy it was my last day in Vegas. Tasha and I had pizza for breakfast then gambled for a couple of hours. She went to her meeting, and I went to the Strip. I gambled up and down the Strip from 1:30 to 9:30 before heading to the airport.

Post 360 2009 Thoughts

That first U.S. leg of the 360 tour in 2009 was really great. I had recaptured that U2 tour love I had on Elevation that I missed on Vertigo. Out of the eight 360 shows I saw, the Vegas show was definitely my favorite with DC, Oklahoma and the first Chicago show as close seconds. For me, how I rank a U2 show is more than just how the actual U2 concert is, although that's a big part of it. It is also about who I saw the show with, what city we were in, where in the concert we were standing and what happened that day leading up to the show. And if I'm going to be completely honest, what sort of Larry moment I had during the show.

A great thing about the first U.S. leg of 360 was for the first time I got to see U2 in cities I had never seen them in before and obviously visit cities I've never been to. My whole life I had wanted to visit Chicago and go to Wrigley Field. Because of U2, I got to do that and now I love Chicago! I had always wanted to visit Atlanta as well and got to do that. Although I'm not a huge fan of Atlanta, but I am glad I got to visit the Martin Luther King sites. I had never really wanted to go to Oklahoma, but it was cool to see it. And I had been to Las Vegas twice before, so any excuse to go to Vegas. I love Vegas! 360 2009 was also great because I got to see and hang out with a lot of friends that I hadn't really seen since the Elevation Tour, because I wasn't really into the Vertigo Tour.

360 Tour 2010 Postponed

Eight months after that great show in Las Vegas, U2 was supposed to embark on their second U.S. leg of the 360 Tour on June 3, 2010 in Salt Lake City. For this leg of the tour, I had planned to pack up my car and drive, with my dogs, to all 12 U2 shows in the U.S. I had never followed a U2 tour before. I was going to be on the road with U2 for two months traveling across America.

On May 21, 2010, just a few days before I was supposed to leave, U2 announced they were postponing the tour opener in Salt Lake City because Bono had to have emergency back surgery that day. They hinted that more shows would probably be postponed as well. I was shocked because I had no idea Bono's injuries were so severe from his fall off the stage during rehearsals. (Are we seeing a pattern here? Fastforward four and a half years to *Songs of Innocence*.) After getting over the shock of how serious Bono was hurt, I had to rework my road trip. Luckily, I wasn't going to lose any money because I was driving everywhere (no flights to cancel) and my hotel reservations were changeable with no charge. I was also lucky because I had the free time to go to the shows no matter when U2 rescheduled them as I wasn't working at the time.

Three days later, it was announced the Glastonbury Festival in England on June 24th was looking for a replacement for U2 and Bono was going home to Ireland to recuperate. This did not bode well for the 360 Tour, so I decided it was time to make a Plan B. I had planned to drive out Route 66 to get to the U2 shows out West. Hoping U2 would not cancel the whole tour, I decided to start my Route 66 trip in a few days as scheduled. This would bring me to Arizona by June 2 putting me in the vicinity to get to the U2 shows in Anaheim, then I could go on with my U2 trip as scheduled. If U2 cancelled the tour, I could continue on with my Route 66 trip.

The next day, on May 25th, I woke up at 7am inundated with news about Bono and the U2 tour. Bono's condition was much more serious than we had originally thought. He was going to need at least eight weeks of rehabilitation. The entire North American leg of the 360 Tour was postponed until 2011. I was supposed to leave the next day. Instead of sitting home and sulking, I decided to get on the road anyway – just not with U2. I drove over to Tulsa to get on Route 66 and drove it out to Albuquerque stopping at all the sites along the way (like Cadillac Ranch). Then after Albuquerque, I drove back through Texas visiting Lubbock (home of Buddy Holly), San Antonio, Austin and Dallas (home of Southerfork!). It was a great trip, but I would have to wait another year to go on the road with U2.

360 (2011)

Bono and Me Seattle June 2011
(Photo by Yarrex Thomas)

Pursuing My Passion on the U2 360 U.S. Tour 2011

Why am I taking this road trip with my dogs for two and a half months across America to all 16 U.S. U2 shows? How can I afford this? How do I have the time to do it? These are some of the questions I was asked over and over while planning and during the 360 Tour. It all started in July 2008 when I quit my well paying stable job in Maryland, leaving my family and friends, to move to Memphis for a less paying less stable job where I knew no one - just because I loved Memphis. This was the first step in pursuing my passion, basically throwing logic and responsibility out the door and just doing what I enjoy.

Step two was when I quit my job at the National Civil Rights Museum a year later. I liked my job and I was finally actually somewhat using my history degree, but it was a $9.25/hour job that wasn't leading anywhere. Plus they weren't going to give me all the days off I needed for the first leg of the U.S. 360 Tour. I had enough in my savings from the sale of my house in Baltimore to last me a couple of years, so I thought why not quit working and just do what I want to do while I am still able to do it. That's exactly what I did. I made a list of all the places I had always wanted to visit but never had. Every other day or so I would visit a place and check it off my list. Sometimes it was a local site like the Dixon Gallery and Gardens in Memphis, sometimes it was a day trip like the Clinton Presidential Library in Little Rock and sometimes it was a weekend trip like to Biloxi, Mississippi. Then in the Fall of 2009, it was the twelve-day road trip on the U2 360 Tour.

Step three was when I saw a documentary called *10MPH* by Hunter Weeks in April 2010. This film inspired me, and made me feel a little less crazy about my decision. Hunter and his friends quit their high-paying corporate jobs, risking financial stability, to pursue their passion of making documentaries. For their first documentary *10MPH*, they filmed their travels across America on segways. It was mentioned in the film that life is too short not to take these risks and adventures when they arise. For me, the risk was financial and the adventure that arose was the U2 360 Tour. It was after watching *10MPH* that I decided to go to every U.S. U2 show on the last leg of the 360 Tour in 2011 and see as much of America along the way as I could, leaving my house and going on the road with U2 for two and a half months for my U2 Tour Across America.

On the Road to Denver

Day 1 – May 14, 2011

My dogs, Elvis and Cilla, and I left Memphis Saturday May 14 at 9:45am CST. We passed through Bono, Arkansas about two hours later, which was a nice reminder of our two and a half month trip we had ahead of us. There was a lot of construction, but luckily not a lot of traffic since it was Saturday. We drove north up Route 63 through small towns that had "filling stations." We travelled through the Ozarks and stopped for the night at a Motel 6 in Independence, Missouri right outside of Kansas City. It was a cold 52 degrees, windy and cloudy. We had driven 455 miles and it was 5:54pm CST. I ordered a pizza from Minsky's, which claimed to be KC's best since 1976, and it was very good and very cheesy. I had the idea of getting pizza in every city I stopped and doing a comparison and contrast sort of thing, but that didn't really happen.

Day 2 – May 15, 2011

The next morning we left Independence, Missouri at 6:30am to drive about three hours north on Route 29 through Iowa to Omaha, Nebraska. It was a nice, easy drive passing by Kauffman Field (KC Royals baseball) and Arrowhead Stadium (KC Chiefs football). I was meeting my Mom and Aunt Pauline in Omaha. They were going to be with me for the first two weeks of my trip. They were not going to the U2 concerts, just along for the sightseeing. Me, my two dogs, my mom and my aunt with all of our luggage (mine for two and a half months worth) in my car for two weeks! Now that's togetherness!

I arrived in Omaha just after 9:30am, got settled into the Sleep Inn and Suites hotel by the airport and waited for Mom and Aunt Pauline's plane to arrive. We went to this cute little section of downtown Omaha called Old Market Square. It was a really cool place with lots of shops, bars and restaurants with cobblestone streets. We had a great lunch at Upstream Brewing Company. I had a really great Reuben Sandwich, which apparently started in Nebraska. I hadn't eaten meat in over a year, but when traveling, I like to eat the local cuisine, or pizza. After lunch, we went back to the hotel to relax.

A few hours later, we went back to Old Market Square for dinner because it was the only place we knew how to get to and it was close. We ate at the Twisted Fork, and I had a cheeseburger. I felt guilty, but it sure tasted better than a veggie burger. I was in cattle country so when in Rome, or Nebraska. It was tough night in that hotel room in Omaha. Only Mom, Elvis and Cilla slept. My aunt and I talked, ate, read and watched tv. Luckily this was the only night we would all be sharing a room, or so we thought.

Day 3 – May 16

      We left Omaha Monday morning at 8am, stopped at Subway in Iowa for breakfast, a Cracker Barrel in Sioux Falls for lunch and then arrived at our hotel the President's View Resort in Keystone, South Dakota 548 miles later at 5:30pm MST. Our hotel overlooked the town of Keystone, which looked like an old western town. From my Mom and Aunt Pauline's balcony, we could see Mount Rushmore in the distance. Mount Rushmore was the first place I planned on visiting on this trip since I first planned it back in 2010. My room was around the other side of the hotel on the first floor, which were the pet rooms. After settling in, we drove down the steep hill to Keystone and had dinner at the Railroad Family Restaurant in Keystone, which was not very good.

Day 4 – May 17

      I got a great night's sleep, a solid, uninterrupted six hours. It was light out at 5am and cold, windy and rainy. We had breakfast at 1880 Keystone House down the hill. It was an ok buffet, but cheap, quick and close – my favorite. If I was alone, I would just eat a cereal bar and be on my way, but Mom and Aunt Pauline like real meals in real restaurants.

      After breakfast, we were off to Mount Rushmore! I was so excited! We arrived, I looked up and it was just magnificent! It was everything I thought it would be and more. I love when I'm not disappointed in the things I have been looking forward to and built up in my mind. I took so many pictures of every angle possible of Mt. Rushmore. There is a park around Mt. Rushmore called Presidents' Trail. We walked all the way around, even my Mom with her bad back and legs. I was wearing my U2 'I'll Go Crazy' shirt with the four faces of U2 on it. A guy stopped me to ask if I was wearing a Mt. Rushmore shirt – because it sort of looked like the faces on Mt. Rushmore. Well that gave me the idea to take a picture of me wearing the four faces of U2 in front of the four faces of Mt. Rushmore.

There were also shops, museums and a café at Mount Rushmore. I bought many souvenirs, but no tee shirt. I swore I wasn't going to buy any tee shirts on this trip, but I broke that promise to myself later. I bought a keychain, a magnet, a small model of Mount Rushmore and a book about the making of Mount Rushmore. Buying books from everywhere we visited came to be my new souvenir, as were magnets because they are easier to display than keychains, my previous souvenir of choice. We had a great lunch at the café with fantastic customer service. Mount Rushmore should be on everyone's bucket list as it exceeded my expectations all the way around.

Our next stop on the loop in the Black Hills of South Dakota was Crazy Horse. Even though my degree is in history, I didn't know much about Crazy Horse the monument or the person, but found it quite fascinating. Crazy Horse was a Native American war leader of the Oglala Lakota. He fought the U.S. government against encroachments to the Lakota territories, including a victory at the Battle of the Little Bighorn in 1876. The Crazy Horse monument is the largest in the world, and still isn't completed yet. The sculpture was begun by Korczak Ziółkowski in 1948. Ziolkowski made it his life work. When he died in 1982, his family kept working on its completion with no money from the government. We started off our tour of Crazy Horse in the visitor's center, took a bus up to the actual monument, then back down to the museum and gift shop. I bought books, a magnet and a Christmas ornament.

We decided to, or really I decided to, continue the loop around back to our hotel through Custer National Park rather than turn around and backtrack the way we come. I thought we would see more that way. We surely did. It was the scariest, windiest, loneliest drive – or so we thought. We drove for what seemed like hours in the middle of nowhere through hairpin turns. We didn't see any other cars. We did see buffalo though. And one looked me right in the eye and was going to charge the car. I was freaking out, so I did a 360 and got out of there quickly.

After a lot of tears and laughter, we finally made it back to our hotel. And to my surprise, Elvis and Cilla were fine and no one complained that they barked while we were gone all day. This was a huge relief to me because that was my only concern about this three months road trip, but now I knew I could leave Elvis and Cilla in the hotel room all day and they would be fine.

We went down the hill to Keystone for dinner to Ruby's Brothel. It was a great restaurant that used to be a brothel and still had red velvet on the walls. The food was fantastic. I had the most amazing salmon en croute. Wow!

Day 5 – May 18

The next day we decided to go to Deadwood and Sturgis. I didn't care what we did after visiting Mount Rushmore. We had breakfast at that same little restaurant with the ok buffet and we were off to Deadwood, which was not what I thought it was going to be. In my mind, I pictured it as this old western town, and it sort of was but a little too modern. We first stopped at the Mount Moriah Cemetery where Wild Bill Hickock and Calamity Jane were buried. It was a great old cemetery. I don't know why I'm so attracted to cemeteries – maybe it's the history. I again bought a book about the history of Deadwood and Mount Moriah as my souvenirs. The cemetery overlooked Deadwood. We drove down and parked in a garage and walked to all the casinos, bars and restaurants. We played the slots at Bullock's Hotel and Casino. I didn't want to play too much, or lose too much, as we were going to be spending five days in Reno soon. We went to Saloon #10 where Wild Bill Hickock was shot. I bought a tee shirt at the Harley Davidson store. This is what started my downfall of buying tee shirts as souvenirs, but this one was blue and orange so I had to get it. We had lunch at Miss Kitty's Cantina, which was in Miss Kitty's Gambling Saloon. Miss Kitty was the Belle of Deadwood, and she also has the same name as my mother.

We left Deadwood for Sturgis, which is the destination of the great annual motorcycle rally. It wasn't much of a town when there is no motorcycle rally though. We went to the Knuckle Bar, and I bought a magnet. We got back to Keystone and again ate dinner at our favorite Ruby's Brothel. I again had the salmon en croute, and it was again fantastic! We walked around the shops after dinner. I bought a great turquoise and orange silver ring, which I wore the rest of my trip and it matched the turquoise in my straw cowboy hat I wore to every U2 show.

Day 6 – May 19

The next morning we left Keystone, South Dakota at 8:45am. We drove for ten minutes, the temperature dropped to 32 degrees and it started snowing. We had lunch in Wheatland, Wyoming at this great little local diner – because Mom and Aunt Pauline can't eat at Subway. We arrived in Denver, Colorado 456 miles later around 5:30pm. We went to check Mom and Aunt Pauline into their hotel, but it was gross, so we cancelled it and they came with me. I could see my hotel, but couldn't figure out how to get to it. It was off the same exit as the stadium, so I pulled into the stadium to ask. I heard the music from U2's 1983 Red Rocks concert coming from Invesco Field. I thought they might play it as U2 walked to the stage on Saturday, but they didn't.

We finally found my hotel, the really cool, circular, Hotel VQ right next to the stadium, literally in the same parking lot. I got out of the car and screamed, scaring both my mom and aunt. I heard the crew sound checking "Zooropa" and then as I continued to unpack the car I heard "Even Better Than the Real Thing," "City of Blinding Lights" and "Streets." We couldn't find Mom and Aunt Pauline a room that night, so they stayed with me and the dogs. It was to be another sleepless night for me, but I didn't care because the U2 show wasn't until the day after next. Plus I was in Denver at the stadium where my beloved Broncos play, and it was my first U2 show of this leg of the tour! All was good in the world. Mom and Aunt Pauline went up to the hotel restaurant for dinner and drinks and brought me back something as I was too tired and stinky to go out in public.

Day 7 – May 20

Because I couldn't sleep, I took the dogs for a walk around the stadium at 6am. I was SO excited to walk around Mile High stadium where my beloved Denver Broncos play! The GA line had already started – right in front of our hotel. I was not getting in line though. I learned back in 2009 there was really no point to it for me. Plus, I wanted to enjoy Denver and spend time with my mom and aunt. We had breakfast in the hotel restaurant. A lady from a radio station in Salt Lake City heard about my trip and wanted to interview me on her radio station. So I called her and she interviewed me on the phone for a few minutes. I never got to hear the interview, but it did air later that day.

After breakfast, we drove into downtown Denver and checked Mom and Aunt Pauline into a nice hotel that I had booked overnight when I wasn't sleeping. We walked around 16th Street Mall, which is just a bunch of shops and restaurants. I really love Denver. If it wasn't so cold there with all that snow, I could live there. We had lunch at the Paramount Café. I went to the Hard Rock to get Dad a pin and noticed all of these people sitting outside. They were U2 fans in line for free tickets. The first 300 people who donated shoes to Soles for Souls got a free ticket to the U2 show. I was to see this again in Seattle and Hollywood.

After lunch, Mom and Aunt Pauline continued to walk around Denver while I went back to my hotel. I walked Elvis and Cilla to the GA line, which had moved around the corner from the hotel. Elvis and Cilla had their U2 laminates that I made for them. They weren't mingling too well with everyone though. This was all very new for them. I saw Jennifer and Melissa and met Beth, who became a good friend on 360. We saw several shows together. I went back to the room to take a nap and do laundry.

That night I drove back into downtown Denver, parked at Mom's hotel and she and I walked over to the Hard Rock for the Under a Blood Red Sky U2 tribute show. My new friend Mark saved us a table right up front by the stage. We had dinner. I had a really great mac and cheese. We met Billy, the Bono of the group, and Jerry, the Larry of the group. They put on a very passionate performance. I also met Chris and Jennifer, who I became friends with and hung out with again at the Baltimore, Chicago and Pittsburgh shows.

My mom was miserable because the music was so loud. It actually seemed louder than an actual U2 show. We left before the first set even ended. When I arrived back to my hotel, I found out U2 had played a secret private concert. I could have stayed at my hotel and listened to the real U2 and maybe caught a glimpse of Larry driving in and out. Oh well.

U2 show #60 – May 21, 2011 – Denver

On Day 8 of my U2 360 Tour across America and the first show of the final leg of the U2 360 Tour, I woke up at 7am and looked out my hotel window to see the GA line. I went to the hotel restaurant to use their WiFi to upload videos and then took lunch back to my room. I walked Elvis and Cilla over to the GA line to hang out for a bit. I saw my old Elevation friends and met some new U2 friends, then we went back to the room and rested for a while.

Leaving Elvis and Cilla safely in the hotel room, I walked back over to the stadium around 4pm to wait for U2 to arrive. As I walked up the hill, the wind almost blew my hat off. It got really cold, so I bought a U2 hoodie. Thank goodness I did because I would wear that sweatshirt at the next five shows. Bono and Edge arrived after 5:30. They stopped and signed, but there were too many people for me to get close to them. Besides, I saw a car waiting down the drive, and I knew it was Larry. It was, but he didn't stop or even roll down the window and wave – this was to be my fate for the next 15 shows.

I walked in the GA entrance after 6pm, no line, no stress. I was heading to Adam's side of the inner circle as was my habit in '09, but I saw my oldest U2 friend from high school Mike, and we decided to go over to Edge's side. It was great to be at Invesco Field at Mile High standing on the actual field where my beloved Denver Broncos play football and then to look up and see John Elway's and Shannon Sharpe's names in the ring of honor. Local band The Fray opened, but I didn't really care for them.

I went behind the stage to wait for U2 to walk in, as I would do for all the shows. In 2009, U2 walked up the stairs to the stage, but for this leg, they walked beside the stairs on Edge's side and underneath the stage. So I was very close to them as they walked by. I yelled for Larry, as I would do for all the shows, and he looked at me, smiled and nodded. I almost cried. Little did I know what more was to come in the next two and a half months. I followed Larry around, as I would do for all the shows, when his drum kit turned around during "Mysterious Ways" and "Sunday Bloody Sunday" and then when he walked around for "I'll Go Crazy if I Don't Go Crazy Tonight." Larry also smiled and nodded at me during "I'll Go Crazy" and when he was leaving stage when I called out his name. It was nice to be able to move around rather than stuck to one spot as I had been in 2009 and past tours. And surprisingly Bono and Edge came behind the stage quite a bit.

The Denver show was great, but I was surprised the audience wasn't that into it. I thought they would be crazy since it was the first show in the US, and I thought Broncos fans were loud, but maybe Broncos fans aren't U2 fans. Tim Tebow was at the show. I didn't see him, but Bono said he was 'in the house.' It was a great set list, except my favorite song "I Still Haven't Found What I'm Looking For" was left out – and would be for the next several shows. But I was SO excited to hear "Pride" back in the set list, so much so that I think it has to be put back into my top five favorite U2 songs. My over excited reaction even surprised me. I heard "Zooropa" and "Scarlet" for the first time ever. I liked how they reworked the shows with so many *Achtung Baby* songs in the beginning, but felt sorry for the folks who didn't get to hear all the new songs off *No Line on the Horizon*.

During the opener "Even Better Than the Real Thing," Bono said, "One Mile," for the Mile High city of Denver. I have never been a big fan of "Even Better," but I love it as the opener and the beginning of it with just Larry on stage banging those drums! U2 tried a remix of "Magnificent" with samples of Bishop Tutu and what sounded like a gospel choir to which Bono said, "it's in development." During "Mysterious Ways," Larry and his drum kit turned around to face the back and Bono said, "Mile High Colorado." I like this song so much better live, especially with the "Yeah! Yeah! Yeah!" at the beginning. I like most U2 songs better live, but some are just SO much better. During "Until the End of the World," Bono gave a little end of the world speech because that night May 21, 2011 was supposed to be the end of the world. Bono said he would be alright as long as Larry Mullen, Adam Clayton and the Edge were with him. Me too Bono, me too. It was also the same date the year before when Bono had his back surgery. Now he was self proclaimed Bono 2.0.

During the band introductions, Bono said, "Part terminator, part Duracell bunny. On the drums, Larry Mullen Jr!" Before "Beautiful Day," Bono brought up three sisters wearing 'Larry Mullen Band' shirts and they read a poem. This sort of bugged me because I know those girls didn't have those shirts 10 years ago when Paola made ours. At the end of the poem, Bono said, "I'm in the Larry Mullen Band." At the end of "Beautiful Day," Bono said, "Rocky Mountain! Colorado!" and then sang a bit of "Here Comes the Sun." During "Zooropa" and "City of Blinding Lights," U2 wore black jackets, except Adam's was white, that lit up. It was really cool and Larry looked hot in his black leather jacket, like he was right out of the 1950s. As if he needs to look any hotter?! After the shock wore off from being so close to Larry during the beginning of "I'll Go Crazy" and he was out of my reach, I was very excited to hear snippets of "Discotheque" and "Please." During "Sunday Bloody Sunday," Larry and his drum kit again turn to face the back and Bono said, "Where's Red Rocks?

Right here." Before "Moment of Surrender," Bono introduced Dallas, brought him on stage and maked him take a bow.

The set list for the first show in the U.S. on the last leg of the 360 tour in Denver on May 21, 2011 was as follows: Even Better Than the Real Thing, I Will Follow, Get on Your Boots, Magnificent remix, Mysterious Ways, Elevation, Until the End of the World, All I Want is You, Stay, Beautiful Day / Here comes the Sun, Pride, Miss Sarajevo, Zooropa, City of Blinding Lights, Vertigo, I'll Go Crazy if I Don't Go Crazy Tonight / Discotheque / Please, Sunday Bloody Sunday, Scarlet, Walk On / You'll Never Walk Alone, One / Will You Still Love Me Tomorrow, Where the Streets Have No Name, Hold Me Thrill Me Kiss Me Kill Me, With or Without You, Moment of Surrender.

Day 9 – May 22

I didn't get much sleep the night after my first U2 show – not surprising. I went up to the hotel restaurant and had breakfast, blogged and uploaded my videos and pictures. Then I drove into downtown Denver to pick up Mom and Aunt Pauline to go to Red Rocks. I had been once before back in 1998 when I visited Denver, but I just went to the amphitheater. I didn't know about the museum, visitor's center and gift shop. So this time we visited everything. We didn't walk down to the stage though, just stood up top and looked down. It's so beautiful at Red Rocks. It would have been amazing to have been there on June 5, 1983 when U2 played, but I was only 10 and didn't even know who they were then. I again got a magnet and tee shirt for souvenirs. No books this time. I couldn't find any. On our way back from Red Rocks, we stopped in the little town of Morrison and had lunch at TNT. It was a cute little town along a stream with lots of motorcycles.

On the Road to Salt Lake City

Day 10 – May 23

The next morning we left Denver at 9:20am and spent most of our day driving through Wyoming. First, we stopped in the smallest town in the United States, Buford – population one. We met the one guy who lives there and runs the store and gas station. He has been featured on many television news shows. From there, we drove to Laramie and had lunch at Perkins. After lunch, we hit some pretty serious hail before coming upon the beautiful mountains outside of Salt Lake City. We arrived at our hotel Homestead Suites at 7:20pm. Normally we would eat somewhere indigenous to the area, but we just had dinner at the Olive Garden because it was the only restaurant close by. Ten hours is a long day driving, and we didn't feel like searching for somewhere to eat.

U2 show #61 – May 24, 2011 – Salt Lake City

Day 11 of my U2 360 Tour Across America had my mom, aunt and myself exploring a bit of Salt Lake City before the U2 show that night. My mom and Aunt Pauline really wanted to see the canyons of Salt Lake City. All I was concerned about was the U2 show that night. We drove past Rice Eccles Stadium at the University of Utah where the show was going to be that night – it was only a few miles from the hotel. It seemed as if we drove around forever searching for canyons to see. We finally stumbled upon Emigration Canyon and had lunch at Ruth's Diner, which had been there since 1930. It was a great place with the best macaroni and cheese I think I ever had, although my stomach didn't really agree.

Never a good idea to eat rich food before a concert, especially standing on the floor at a U2 show.

Mom and Aunt Pauline stayed at the hotel relaxing and doing their laundry while I went to the U2 show. I left at 3pm, drove a few miles and realized I didn't have my ticket. I had to turn around and go back and get it. This was one of only three times that I drove to a U2 show out of the 16 shows that leg. Something happened at this U2 show that has never happened to me before – free parking! The University of Utah had free parking for the U2 concert. I couldn't believe it. Of course I had to walk about 20 minutes through campus to get to Rice Eccles Stadium. It was just about 4pm when I happened upon the GA line. I started to talk to people, so I decided to just stay in the line. This was the only time this leg of the tour that I got in the GA line and did not wait for U2 to arrive. I met up with my new friend Jason. We met up at a few more shows along the tour, Nashville and Minneapolis.

Once inside, I went to Adam's side of the inner circle, but by 7pm it was so crowded I couldn't even get into my pocket to take out my camera, so I decided to move. I walked around the stadium while The Fray played. I went into the stands to get a drink. I ran into Mike again and my old Elevation friends Matt and Melissa. I went over to Edge's side of the inner circle to watch U2 walk in and then went back over to Adam's side to watch the show. During "Walk On," I went back to soundboard and watched the rest of the show from there. This is was the only show I didn't watch U2 leave the stage from the back. I didn't get any Larry love in Salt Lake City, no smiles, nods or waves.

Salt Lake City was a good show, but the audience still wasn't that into it, not like I remember from 2009. Maybe people are just more mellow in Denver and Salt Lake City. U2 entered and it was still light out, which was very cool and the first time I had experienced that. During the opener "Even

Better Than the Real Thing," Bono said "beautiful Utah!" Bono said, "Bass and Drums!" during "Until the End of the World" as he would at a few shows. This really excited me! Bono really didn't do band introductions, he just talked about how a lot had changed since 2009 with Adam becoming a father and Larry acting in a movie. Bono then went on to make fun of Larry saying he is going to star in a Billy Idol biopic this summer, after Billy cleaned up. Larry really thought that was funny and cracked up.

    I really missed "I Still Haven't Found What I'm Looking For." I like "All I Want is You" and was excited to hear it in Denver because I hadn't heard it in a while, but it is no replacement for "Still Haven't Found." "All I Want is You" is a love song, not an uplifting song like "Still Haven't Found." It is just not a fair trade. The highlight of this show by far was "Love Rescue Me," even if it was only a few lines. I cried, but luckily I had the presence of mind to video it. "Love Rescue Me" is my second favorite song from my second favorite album "Rattle and Hum," and I had never heard it live before. It was Bob Dylan's birthday, which is why U2 played it and after we sang "Happy Birthday" to Bob Dylan. Bono again brought up the 'three sisters' to read the poem before "Beautiful Day." Bono commented how they have been on the road with U2 seeing 10 shows. I wasn't impressed. During "I'll Go Crazy If I Don't Go Crazy Tonight," Bono said "Salt Lake City on a Tuesday night I know where we can take this," and U2 played snippets of "Discotheque" and "Mofo" instead of "Please." Bono introduced the band after "Moment of Surrender" just before they left the stage.

    The set list for the 360 show in Salt Lake City on May 24, 2011 was as follows: Even Better Than the Real Thing, I Will Follow, Get on Your Boots, Magnificent remix, Mysterious Ways, Elevation, Until the End of the World, All I Want is You / Love Rescue Me / Happy Birthday, Stay, Beautiful Day / Here

Comes the Sun, Pride, Miss Sarajevo, Zooropa, City of Blinding Lights, Vertigo, I'll Go Crazy / Discotheque / Mofo, Sunday Bloody Sunday, Scarlet, Walk On / You'll Never Walk Alone, One, Blowin in the Wind / The Times They Are a Changin / Where the Streets Have No Name, Hold Me Thrill Me Kiss Me Kill Me, With or Without You, Moment of Surrender.

Day 12 – May 25

     The day after the U2 show in Salt Lake City, we toured around Temple Square in downtown Salt Lake City. We parked at the Joseph Smith Building, which reminded me a lot of The Peabody in Memphis. Joseph Smith started the Mormon church. Right next to the Joseph Smith building was the Brigham Young statue. Brigham Young brought the Mormon church to Salt Lake City after Joseph Smith was killed. We went through the south visitor center where I learned all of this. There was a model of the Temple, since we weren't allowed inside the actual Temple.

     Next we went to Assembly Hall, which is a small church. We saw the Christest statue in the north visitor center. We attended the Tabernacle Organ Recital, which was really beautiful. We went on top of the building where there was a huge garden that overlooked the city and even had a waterfall down the front of the building. Then we went back to the Joseph Smith building and had lunch at the Garden Café on the 10th floor. It was nice to see all the sights at Temple Square in Salt Lake city, but it wasn't anything too exciting. Although Salt Lake City had some of the most beautiful views – everywhere you looked snowcapped mountains. Simply beautiful! After our tiring day, we just went back to our hotel and relaxed after getting some groceries at Whole Foods. I got pizza to try to start up my pizza in every city quest.

On the Road to Seattle

Day 13 – May 26

My mom, Aunt Pauline, Elvis, Cilla and I piled in the car once again and left Salt Lake City for Reno, Nevada. Eight hours later, we arrived at the Ramada Reno Hotel and Casino, where we would stay for the next five nights. We were so happy to stay in the same place for more than a couple nights. I really liked our hotel, which had a restaurant and small casino, as well as a really nice big room. I wanted to stay on the strip, but no hotels allowed two dogs. Of course I would have rather been in Las Vegas than Reno, but Reno was on the way from Salt Lake City to Seattle.

Day 14 – May 27

We had a yummy breakfast in the hotel restaurant before taking the free hotel shuttle a mile down the road to the Reno strip for a day of gambling. We played the slots at Eldorado, Silver Legacy, Circus Circus and Harrah's. I won a little bit, but ended up about even for the day. We had lunch at Café Sedona at Silver Legacy. After about 6 hours on the Reno strip, we took the hotel shuttle back and had dinner in the hotel restaurant and gambled a little more in the hotel casino. I did not love Reno. It was a bit ghetto, nothing like Vegas.

Day 15 – May 28

We started out our day just like yesterday, with a yummy filling breakfast in our hotel. But that's where the similarity ended. This 15th day of my U2 360 Tour Across America brought me, my mom and my aunt through Carson City and into the snow of Lake Tahoe. Our first stop was just about 10-15 minutes from our hotel, south of Reno on the way to Carson City and Lake Tahoe. We stopped at the Chocolate Nugget Candy Factory. I think I bought enough candy to last me for the rest of my U2 360 road trip – peanut butter fudge, chocolate covered graham crackers, chocolate caramels and a big hunk of white chocolate. We made it to Carson City and just drove through and see what it was like. There was a casino and a couple of cool looking bars and a park, but not a big vacation destination.

     By the time we reached Lake Tahoe, the temperature had drastically dropped. It was about 50 degrees when we left Reno and it dropped into the 30s by the time we stopped at Lake Tahoe to take pictures. We drove around the Lake and went into the Horizon Casino. I wanted to stop there because it used to be the Sahara Casino where Elvis performed in the 1970s. There was no longer any evidence of the King though. We decided rather than drive back the way we came, to drive all the way around Lake Tahoe – so we could see everything. It seemed every time we decide to 'drive all the way around' rather than backtrack, we got into trouble. We made our way into California along Route 89. This road was quite narrow and at many points had no guard rail and just dropped off with no shoulder. My mom was terrified and at one pointed shouted, "Stop the car and let me out!" After, she didn't even remember saying it she was so scared. To make matters worse, it was snowing. Not just flurries, a real hard snow. I could not believe it was 32 degrees and snowing on Memorial Day Weekend, the official start of summer. I never thought it would be this cold on my summer road trip, or that I would encounter snow twice! We made it back to our hotel and stayed there the rest of the night, having dinner at the hotel restaurant.

Day 16 – May 29

  The next morning we started off our Sunday at Peg's Glorified Ham and Eggs for breakfast. Apparently it is the must-eat breakfast spot. It was definitely a local spot, not a lot of tourists there. It lived up to its name for me. Breakfast was fantastic and they had fresh squeezed orange juice. After breakfast, the sleet/snow/rain had stopped and we headed out to the Grand Sierra Resort. We noticed this casino on our way to Lake Tahoe the day before. The Grand Sierra Hotel and Casino is only about a mile from our hotel and about a mile from downtown Reno. I would definitely stay there if I ever get back to Reno. The hotel allows dogs and is reasonably priced! It was the best casino I saw in Reno, reminded me a bit of Dover Downs. Grand Sierra has a great variety of slots and several bars and restaurants, so there is no real need to ever leave the resort. Besides free drinks, they were also giving out free cookies!

Day 17 – May 30

  The next day before taking Mom and Aunt Pauline to the airport for their noon flight home, we had breakfast in our hotel and then went back to the fabulous Grand Sierra Resort to gamble for a couple hours. After I dropped them off at the airport, I went to Petco to get dog food for Elvis and Cilla, got gas for our trip tomorrow, and went to Subway for lunch. I was back at the hotel by 1, and Elvis, Cilla and I just relaxed for the rest of the day before our long drive to Portland the next day. Part one of my U2 360 Tour Across America had ended.

Day 18 – May 31

  The day after my mom and aunt left, Elvis, Cilla and I left Reno at 6:30am and finally arrived in Portland, Oregon 715 miles later at 6:30pm. I took the long way, so I could drive on bigger roads – 80 west to 5 north. It was beautiful scenery between the rain and fog up and down the mountains. I stopped just twice on our 12 hour drive listening to U2 the entire way, as I would do for the rest of my trip since my mom and aunt were no longer with me. When I got to the fabulous Vintage Plaza hotel in Portland, there was a welcome sign for Elvis and Cilla, they had upgraded us to a huge suite, and gave me free valet parking. In our beautiful suite, *How to Dismantle an Atomic Bomb* was already playing in the cd player and there was a framed picture of Elvis and Cilla. I had a bottle of wine waiting for me as well as vouchers for the restaurant and honor bar. Elvis and Cilla had all sorts of treats waiting for them as well.

Day 19 – June 1

My stay at the Hotel Vintage Plaza in Portland got better and better. I literally made my upgraded luxurious suite our haven for 36 hours, only going outside to take Elvis and Cilla to O'Bryant Square. It was nice just to do nothing after almost 3 weeks of going and going. I used my restaurant vouchers and ordered lunch and dinner in my room. It was fantastic! I loved Portland. Even though I only saw the couple blocks around my hotel, it seems like my kind of city – big enough where there is plenty to do and very liberal and dog friendly.

Day 20 – June 2

Upon my checkout of the Hotel Vintage Plaza, Jonathan, who had checked me in, left me *All That You Can't Leave Behind* cd for my drive to Seattle. On my way to my car, I met Jeri, the General Manager, and her dog Georgie, Diva of Pet Relations. Jeri contacted all the Kimpton hotels I was going to be staying at (Seattle, Miami, Chicago, Philadelphia) asking them to treat me well. Kimpton Hotels is now my favorite hotel brand. They have the best customer service I've ever seen and are truly dog friendly. They is no charge extra for dogs nor do they have breed or size restrictions. They also provide dog snacks, toys and bowls.

After passing by the Tacoma Dome, where I saw U2 10 years prior on the Elevation Tour, and passing by Qwest Field, where U2 is playing on this 360 tour, we arrived at the Monaco Hotel in Seattle around 12:30pm. My old Elevation friend Jenny joined us for our stay in Seattle, which was to be one of the best times of my entire trip. In fact, my time in Seattle began my favorite part of my U2 360 tour – from Seattle to Oakland to Anaheim to Baltimore. Not my favorite U2 shows necessarily, but my favorite part of traveling.

My old Elevation friend Jenny met me in Seattle. We went to the North American premiere of *Killing Bono* at the Seattle International Film Festival. It was shown at the Neptune Theatre, one of the University District's oldest theatres. The movie *Killing Bono* is based on Neil McCormick's memoir *Killing Bono: I was Bono's Doppelganger.* I liked the book better. In *Killing Bono*, Neil McCormick tells the story of his life and how he was always competing, in his mind, with U2. He went to school with Bono, Larry, Adam and Edge and was forming a band at the same time they were. In fact, his brother Ivan was almost in U2. Ivan was in Larry's kitchen at that first rehearsal. Neil always wanted to be famous and be in the biggest band in the world, but that happened to Bono not him.

The movie *Killing Bono* was good. It was well-done, entertaining and funny. I especially liked Robert Sheehan who played Ivan McCormick, Neil's brother. I liked that the only U2 song that was played in the movie was my favorite "I Still Haven't Found What I'm Looking For," especially since I'm wasn't hearing it at the concerts at the time. The Larry character of course did not do Larry justice, but the Adam's character late 1970s hair was spot on. What I did not like was that the movie took some liberties with the truth and added scenes for dramatic purposes that did not happen. One of these scenes was Neil McCormick pointing a gun at Bono deciding if he was going to kill him. It was very disturbing. All I kept thinking was 'Mark Chapman.' The book *Killing Bono* had more U2 in it, especially when they were starting out, and continued throughout Neil McCormick's writing career, past 1987 where the movie ended.

After the showing, director Nick Hamm skyped in and did a Q & A with the audience. He said that U2, with the exception of Larry, viewed *Killing Bono* in Australia when they were touring there. He said they found themselves amusing, especially Adam's hair. I was surprised that the small theatre was only about half full, and that it wasn't all U2 fans. There were some folks there with U2 shirts on, but it was mostly film festival fans. I expected it to be in a huge sold out theatre with wall to wall U2 fans. I mean I changed my plans and came into Seattle a day early just so I could see the North American premiere of *Killing Bono.*

Day 21 – June 3

The next day Jenny and I started with breakfast at the Blue Water Taco Grill. I had a yummy veggie scramble. We walked to the Monorail, which was still operating from when it started at the 1961 World's Fair, the same fair where Elvis filmed *It Happened at the World's Fair.* The joy I got from this was a bit over the top, but it's the little things in life. The Monorail took us to the Space Needle, but we didn't go up in it. I went up in it 10 years ago when I was here for U2's Elevation show in Tacoma. Right next to the Space Needle was the Experience Music Project, which was showing a Nirvana exhibit – the reason why I went to the EMP.

The Experience Music Project was named and modeled after Jimmy Hendrix. The Nirvana exhibit was great.

It had memorabilia, photos, performances, documentaries, and a studio where fans could record their Nirvana stories. But I did not record the dreams/nightmares I had after Kurt's death involving me yelling at Courtney. I bought a Kurt Cobain biography, a Nirvana tee shirt, Elvis guitar picks, a drum keychain and Seattle and EMP/Nirvana magnets.

After the EMP, Jenny and I wanted to take a bus tour and had only a short time to make it. While we were rushing to catch the light rail, we heard the drums for "Desire." We paused because we weren't sure we heard it correctly, but then we heard "Lover I'm on the street." So we ran toward "Desire." It was a band and gospel choir on the back of a semi truck. The banner above the stage read "One Life No Regrets" and then in smaller letters "noregretsu2." The singer, Patrick Stark, turned 40 and wanted to make sure he was living his life with no regrets – something I could identify with. He had always had a fear of singing in public, so to conquer his fear he was making a documentary called *One Life No Regrets* about his quest to sing on stage with U2. In preparation, he sang a set of U2 songs with a Gospel choir – "Desire," "In God's Country," "All I Want is You," "One," and "Until the End of the World."

After our impromptu U2 show, Jenny and I walked to Pike Place Market for lunch. We stumbled upon the Hard Rock on our way and people were lined up just like they were at the Denver Hard Rock waiting for free tickets to the U2 concert. They brought shoes to donate to the Souls for Soul charity, and those first 100 people or so were to get free U2 tickets. We went to the Fish Market and saw them throw the fish and then had lunch at the café overlooking the water. I of course had tuna. What else do you have at a fish market?

After lunch it was finally time for our Sub Seattle bus tour, which we had tried to take earlier but got sidetracked by Patrick's U2 show. We lucked out and it was only Jenny and I on the tour. This Sub Seattle tour told us the non-toursity, non-obvious facts about Seattle. We went to Beacon Hill, Washington Lake and my reason on going on the tour Kurt Cobain's house. We also saw the Black Hole Sun sculpture, which supposedly inspired Soundgarden's song. Looking through the hole, you can see the Space Needle in the distance.

After our busy day walking around in the rare Seattle sun, we just relaxed in our hotel room and ordered room service. Seattle is a great city, but very hilly! I loved Seattle. It is a great city with great people, and while I was there the weather was great. My time in Seattle was one of the best times I had on my entire trip.

U2 show #62 – June 4, 2011 – Seattle

Day 22 of my U2 360 Tour Across America was one of my favorites of the summer. The U2 360 show in Seattle was better than the previous two shows I had been to in Denver and Salt Lake City. Even though it was the same set list, the audience was much more into it, the band was having a blast and actually seemed a little more into as well, Lenny Kravitz was a better opening act than The Fray, and oh yeah I talked with Bono before the show about Larry and Larry shook my hand as he was leaving the show.

To conserve energy on that rare sunny day in Seattle on June 4th, Jenny and I took a cab to Qwest Field even though it was just a mile away. We got to the stadium at 3:00, got in the GA line just long enough to get our wristbands and then walked around to wait for U2 to arrive. We met some new folks and talked with old friends. I met Chuck and Michelle whom I've stayed friends with. Chuck and I would go on to see many other shows together. The people there waiting for U2 told us Larry had just went it, so I was a little disappointed, but they were wrong.

After a short time, we saw the flashing lights of the police escort and black SUVs. Edge, Bono, Adam AND LARRY drove into Qwest Field right in front of us. We looked down the long driveway and saw Bono get out and head back toward us. He hopped on the back of the policeman's motorcycle and in seconds was talking with us. Jenny and I were in our 'Larry Mullen Band' shirts as usual. I shouted, "Is Larry ever coming out to greet the fans ... of the Larry Mullen Band?" Bono responded, "He only likes you. I love you." Everyone laughed. Then Bono went on to say, "You like that kind of cold stare" (referring to Larry). Before Bono was about to leave, he asked the small crowd of about 30 people, "Where are the Larry Mullen people?" I shouted, 'Right here!" and pushed my way toward Bono. He read my shirt as if to make sure I was the 'Larry Mullen Band' girl he had been talking to earlier. Then Bono asked, "Do you have a message I can deliver?" I was confused and frantic. I thought he was going to tell me a message from Larry, but I quickly realized what he had said and I replied, "Yes, tell Larry to come out in Oakland since he didn't come out here." He said, "OK." I then went on to tell him that I would be at all the US shows, but I don't think he heard me. Bono then asked my name and repeated it back to me, "Deena." When he got in his golf cart to go back, I saw him write something down. I was hoping it was my message to Larry. I had no idea what this conversation would eventually lead to almost two months later in Pittsburgh.

After our talk with Bono, we got in the GA line and had about an hour wait in the hot Seattle sun before we were let into Qwest Field. While waiting we got to hear the sound check. I was quite excited to hear "The Fly," but disappointed when it wasn't included in the set list later. Once inside, we got a nice spot in the inner circle on Adam's side – a great view of Lenny Kravitz. Lenny was a great opening act, a lot better than The Fray. He didn't take the stage until 7:30 and only played 45 minutes, but played the four songs I know – "It Ain't Over Til It's Over," "American Woman," "Fly Away," and "Are You Gonna Go My Way." Lenny had these great female backup singers that reminded me of Elvis' Sweet Inspirations. Lenny also did karate moves that reminded me of Elvis. Could Lenny be a fan of The King?

After Lenny Kravitz' performance, we went over to Edge's side and stood behind the stage to wait for U2 to enter. It was odd getting our neck's stamped, instead of our hands, for re-entry to the inner circle, but this was to be the practice for most of the tour. Security kicked us off the rail where we were waiting for U2 to enter, claiming the fire marshall wanted that space cleared. So instead of having us lined up along the rail out of the way of traffic like we were, they had us lined up horizontally sort of blocking the way to the inner circle. Not sure how that wasn't a fire hazard? This was also to happen for most of the tour. But as soon as U2 came out of that tunnel, security couldn't hold us back and we were again on the rail. Larry came by and smiled at me, and I think he may have waved – of course I was screaming his name and wearing my "Larry Mullen Band" shirt, so what else was he going to do? We decided to stay on Edge's side for the show, and it was a good decision. We had a great view. It was side view, but we could see everything.

During "Even Better Than the Real Thing," Bono shouted, "The Emerald City shining in the sun." During "Get on Your Boots" right before my favorite "LET ME IN THE SOUND", Bono said, "Larry Mullen!" Apparently he did this at most shows, but I never heard him because I was too busy screaming. I would get SO excited for "Get on Your Boots"!

Most people hate it, but I love that song!
Before "Magnificent," Bono said, "Here comes the Boss, the Arch" (referring to Arch Bishop Desmin Tutu and his part in the "Magnificent" remix. Before "Until the End of the World," Bono sang, "It's the end of the world as we know it. Edge feels fine." Some folks from REM were apparently at the show, not that I saw them.

During the band introductions, Bono talked about how June 4th was a date we were all going to remember. It certainly was for me, as it was one of my favorite shows of the 360 tour. Bono again mentioned the rare sunny day in Seattle. He said the band was going to start again and we should pretend we didn't know them. Bono said, "You think of him as a tough guy, but he's a very thoughtful man. On the drums, Larry Mullen Jr!" For the first time, video of Commander Kelly at the Space Station is shown before "Beautiful Day." He was holding words from the song and then says, "Tell my wife I love her." Video of Kelly is shown later in the song as he recites the lyrics. Commander Kelly is married to Congresswoman Gabby Gifford who was shot months earlier. This video was played before "Beautiful Day" for the rest of the tour. The audience would get really excited each time he would say their city's name. I don't think they realized it was pre-recorded and he was not actually talking to us from space.

At the end of "Vertigo," we went behind the stage to wait for Larry and his conga to start his walk for "I'll Go Crazy If I Don't Go Crazy Tonight." He again smiled at me as I screamed his name and jumped up and down. I actually think he was laughing at me, but I'll take it. For "Moment of Surrender," we moved behind the stage to wait for U2 to leave. Instead of standing by the stairs at the stage where we could have gotten a good picture, we waited back toward where the tunnel is. As Larry was walking out, Jenny shouted, "Larry!" He smiled and made a b line for us. Larry shook

Jenny's hand and then mine, and he was still smiling. I thanked him. Excited as I was, I thought to myself that this does not excuse Larry from coming out to meet me in Oakland, assuming Bono gave him my message.

After the show as we were walking through the crowded parking lot, we passed by Eddie Vedder and his bodyguard looking for their car. I of course ran after them to try to get a picture, but was unsuccessful. I did manage to snap one just before Eddie was getting into the car, but it was of course blurry and of the back of him.

The set list for the 360 show in Seattle on June 4, 2011 was as follows: Even Better Than The Real Thing, I Will Follow, Get On Your Boots, Magnificent, Mysterious Ways, Elevation, It's the End of the World as We Know It / Until the End of the World / Where Have All the Flowers Gone, All I Want Is You, Stay, Beautiful Day / Space Oddity, Pride, Miss Sarajevo, Zooropa, City of Blinding Lights, Vertigo, I'll Go Crazy / Discotheque /Life During Wartime / Psycho Killer, Sunday Bloody Sunday, Scarlet, Walk On /You'll Never Walk Alone, One / Will You Love Me Tomorrow, Where the Streets Have No Name / All You Need is Love, Hold Me Thrill Me Kiss Me Kill Me, With or Without You, Moment of Surrender.

That Seattle show is still one of my favorites of the 360 tour. It had a much a better energy than the previous two I had seen in Denver and Salt Lake City. Also, it was great to see it with my old Elevation friend Jenny. It was also the show where I met Chuck, whom I saw many shows with on 360. Seattle was where I met and spoke with Bono about meeting Larry and where Larry shook my hand as he left. It was a great night!

On the Road to Oakland

Day 23 – June 5

    Elvis, Cilla and I left Seattle just before 1pm the day after the U2 show in Seattle. We drove to Eugene, Oregon and spent the night at a Motel 6. It was the first time on my trip that I drove to another city the day after the U2 show. I was exhausted, even though I only drove five hours. It was also the first time I drove and it didn't rain.

Day 24 – June 6

    We left Eugene the next morning just before 9am and arrived at La Quinta hotel in Oakland just after 6pm, stopping three times along the way. I was in such a good mood on the drive. I'm not sure if it was a good night's sleep or the memory of Larry's smile walking toward me at the end of that Seattle show that kept me happily on my way. Even the guy at the California inspection was in a good mood that day. He was a U2 fan. He said the U2 trucks came through a few days ago on their way to Oakland.

    I was really happy I was going to be in California for the next 13 days. I really loved traveling out west, especially the west coast. It was definitely my favorite part of my trip. What I didn't like was having to backtrack routes. I drove north on route 5 from Reno to Portland, and then drove south on route 5 from Seattle to Oakland. But that was nothing compared to July when I would go back and forth across the Ohio and PA turnpikes over and over.

    In Oakland I noticed that in addition to this being my U2 360 tour, this was also my tuna and pizza tour. I pretty much lived on tuna and pizza the entire three months, as well as sweet tea and sun chips. I had the best tuna melt I've ever had at the Hotel VQ in Denver, had an ok tuna melt at

Carrow's in Reno, and a great tuna salad sandwich at Pike Place Market in Seattle. In addition, I've had tuna subs from various Subways along the way. I had a yummy pizza in Kansas City my first night on the road. I had pizza from the hotel restaurants at the Ramada Reno, Vintage Plaza Portland, and Monaco Seattle. The best of these was the margherita pizza in Portland.

U2 show #63 – June 7, 2011 – Oakland

The U2 360 show in Oakland had the same set list as the previous three shows in the U.S., but the show was a little different. First, the baseball infield was fenced off, so the GA area was smaller as was the inner circle behind the stage. Second, there were two opening bands, so U2 didn't come on until 9:30. Third, and most important to me, Larry sang!!!

I spent the first half of Day 25 of my U2 360 Tour Across America resting in my hotel room to conserve energy for the U2 show, as I did before every show. My routine was to stay in bed reading and watching tv until about 1pm, take Elvis and Cilla out, eat and shower, and then head over to the stadium around 2 or 3. I would wait for U2 to arrive, then go into the show.

Even though my hotel was less than a mile from McAfee Coliseum, I took the free hotel shuttle over to the Coliseum just after 2:00. I walked around the stadium and arena and finally found my friends, Matt, Melissa and Kim waiting for U2 to arrive. My new friend Barb found us and then I met Paula, who brought me a cool pin and later sent me the review from the Oakland paper and pictures she took at the show. Bono arrived just after 5pm, stopped the car right in front of us and hopped out.

As soon as Bono got out of the car, I pointed at him and then at my "Larry Mullen Band" shirt and said, "Now Bono…" He put his hands in the air and said, "I tried." Then he walked right over to us, and I said, "So he's not coming (referring to Larry)?" Bono again said, "I tried." While he was signing autographs, I told him that it's ok because I'll be at other shows. Bono asked me, "What is your name, Deah?" I said, "Deena." He said, "Yes, I remember." He went on to talk to others. Bono looked tired, his voice was scratchy, and he said he was sick. Before he got back into the car to go inside, Bono looked over to me and shouted, "I'll try again." It was in Oakland that I realized my quest on the 360 tour, besides driving to every U.S. show, was to meet Larry. I thought it would be easy, since Bono had come out to greet the fans at all first four U.S. shows and I had already talked with him twice about meeting Larry. Little did I know that was my last chance to speak with Bono.

I went into the Coliseum in Oakland after 6pm and still got into the inner circle. It was a strange set up though. The baseball infield was fenced off, so the GA section was a lot smaller. And the back of the inner circle behind the stage where I usually stand was a bit narrower as well. Also, there was a wall of empty sky boxes instead of seated fans behind the stage, which made for an echoing drum sound. Because the GA was smaller, the inner circle was more crowded. It was a very laid back crowd though, and it very cold and windy that night. Even Larry wore his hoodie.

There were two opening bands for U2 in Oakland. Local band MoonAlice played from 7:00 to 7:30. I was not impressed. The sound was bad and just not my cup of tea. Lenny Kravitz played from about 7:50 to 8:30. It was the same set list as the previous show in Seattle. Lenny puts on a really great show.

I waited for U2 to enter the Coliseum. They were going to enter from directly behind the stage rather than come around from the side, so I could get great video and pictures of their entrance. As they walked to the stage, Larry looked at me and smiled and waved, and I was actually able to capture it on video without shaking!

The set list in Oakland was the same as the previous three shows in the U.S. with one notable exception, and for me the highlight of the show. Larry sang a part of Lou Reed's "Perfect Day." There were no band introductions at the Oakland show. Instead, Bono talked about the G3 Summit the night before with Greenday and Metallica and the possibility of doing a music festival with them. Edge spoke a bit about it and then Bono asked Larry what else was discussed. Larry said, "What goes on at that summit, stays at that summit." Bono then asked Larry if any individual names came up. Larry responded, "Lou Reed perhaps" and sang a bit of Lou Reed's "Perfect Day," then concluded by saying, "Lou, we love you man." Lou Reed was apparently at the show, not that I saw him. Too bad they didn't do "Satellite of Love." I couldn't believe Larry sang! I was SO excited! I haven't seen Larry sing in concert since ZooTV!

The set list for 360 in Oakland on June 7, 2011 was as follows: Even Better Than The Real Thing, I Will Follow, Get On Your Boots, Magnificent, Mysterious Ways, Elevation, Until the End of the World / Anthem / Where Have All The Flowers Gone, Perfect Day / Happy Birthday, All I Want Is You, Stay, Beautiful Day / Space Oddity, Pride, Miss Sarajevo, Zooropa, City of Blinding Lights, Vertigo, I'll Go Crazy / Discotheque / Life During Wartime / Psycho Killer, Sunday Bloody Sunday, Scarlet, Walk On, One, Will You Love Me Tomorrow – Where the Streets Have No Name, Hold Me Thrill Me Kiss Me Kill Me, With or Without You, Moment of Surrender.

Day 26 – June 8

    The day after the U2 show in Oakland, I just stayed in my hotel room napping, reading, watching television and relaxing. Luckily I had enough leftovers (pizza of course), so I didn't have to go out for food, just to walk the dogs. My hotel here is nice because it has free breakfast, free shuttle to and from the concert, and they delivered a microwave and refrigerator, but the walls are very thin. Every time someone shut a door or talked in the hall, my dogs would bark even at 4am while I was sleeping. I didn't sleep much in Oakland.

Day 27 – June 9

    The next day I drove to Jack London Square in Oakland and took the 9:15am ferry to Fisherman's Wharf in San Francisco. Unfortunately, there were about four large groups of children on field trips on the ferry and it was cloudy and cold when I arrived in San Francisco. Of course it was warming up and sunny as I was leaving to return back to Oakland.

    I spent my time in San Francisco at Fisherman's Wharf, walking up and down and all around. I looked at the historical ships on Hyde Street Pier and had lunch at historic Boudin's (sourdough since 1849). I could barely see the Golden Gate Bridge through the fog, but I could see Alcatraz and some good views of the San Francisco skyline and hilly streets. Luckily, I had been to San Francisco before, so I've seen all the sights.

On the Road to Anaheim

Day 28 – June 10

    The next day we left Oakland around 7:20am, and it was 55 degrees. Just over eight hours later, we arrived in Palm Springs and it was 95 degrees. We only stopped twice on our journey south on Route 5 up and down the mountains, again. It was a pretty drive though. But finally it was summer! For the first time since I left Memphis on May 14th, it was above 75 degrees. In fact, one day in Denver it was above 70 and one day in Seattle above 70, otherwise it was cold. Finally on June 10th, summer had arrived!

I loved Palm Springs! I loved the desert! After my visit, I was seriously considering moving there. The weather is perfect. It is hot, but no humidity so it's cool in the mornings and nights. It is a very dog-friendly town, even restaurants allow them. It is not crowded and seemed clean and safe. Most of the buildings in downtown Palm Springs are very 1960s retro. Our hotel, A Place in the Sun garden hotel is my new favorite hotel. It is named after one of my favorite movies, *A Place in the Sun* starring Elizabeth Taylor, Montgomery Clift, and Shelley Winters. The production crew stayed there while they were filming.

A Place in the Sun hotel is a collection of bungalows situated in a rectangle surrounding the pool with palm trees and mountains in the background. It was gorgeous! It was built in the 1950s, so it was very retro, which I obviously love. There is even a walled in patio, so the dogs had a little space to go off leash. And to make it even better, they upgraded me to a one bedroom bungalow, which is basically like an apartment with a full kitchen, dining room table, two couches and tv in the living room, a king bed, closet, and tv in the bedroom. They even had a library of books and movies for me to enjoy. Elvis and Cilla really enjoyed having an apartment with a patio that they could run around in, rather than being in a small hotel room. Palm Springs was my favorite city I visited on my U2 360 tour across America.

Day 29 – June 11

After a great night's sleep in my lovely bungalow at A Place in the Sun garden hotel, I left by 9am in search for Elvis – well his homes. My first stop was Elvis' home on 845 W Chino Canyon, which he bought in 1970 and owned until he died in 1977. Luckily the owner, Reno, was leaving as I pulled up so we chatted for a bit. He couldn't give me a tour of the house because June is the month he does maintenance. Unfortunately, not much in the house is original because it was broken into four days after Elvis died and then Graceland came and took everything. Reno has lived there for seven years. There was a great metal Elvis sculpture on the front of the house that someone had put up before he moved there.

My next stop had nothing to do with Elvis, but when there is a casino I must play. I went to the Spa Resort Casino and quickly lost my money. It is a very small casino, which did not have my favorite slots. I had lunch at the Oasis Buffet, which was ok, but not as good as the Paula Deen's buffet I was used to at the Casino in Tunica.

Next was the favorite part of my day. I toured Elvis' honeymoon hideaway. Elvis leased this house at 1350 Ladero Circle for a year, and he and Priscilla spent their honeymoon there on May 1, 1967. I had the most wonderful tour of every inch of this gorgeous 1960s house. It was a private tour I scheduled. It was great to see the living room that I had seen in so many pictures. Maria was the best tour guide and as big an Elvis fan as I am. It was a real pleasure to hear her Elvis in Palm Springs stories that I knew nothing about. She told me about Elvis' shopping trips to Rite Aid and what he ate at his favorite restaurant. A visit to Elvis' house is a must for any Elvis fan visiting Palm Springs.

My last stop of the day was the Rite Aid that Maria told me about. I needed to get some groceries anyway since I had a full kitchen, and I would at my hotel in Anaheim as well. So I thought why not pick a few things up where Elvis shopped. And the next day I was going to have lunch at Elvis' favorite restaurant in Palm Springs, Las Casuelas.

Day 30 – June 12

My plan was to make the pilgrimage to THE Joshua Tree, the one U2 was photographed with for my favorite album *The Joshua Tree,* but I realized that it was almost five hours north of Palm Springs on my way from Oakland. I knew it was in the Mohave Desert near Death Valley and was not in Joshua Tree Park, but I thought it was on the way to Joshua Tree National Park. Since I couldn't go to the real Joshua Tree, I went to Harmony Motel, only an hour away, where U2 was also photographed.

U2 stayed at the Harmony Motel while making *The Joshua Tree* album. It is a very small, retro motel. It is a far cry from the five star resort hotels U2 stay at now. Even though I couldn't see THE Joshua Tree, I could see many Joshua Trees at Joshua Tree National Park. It was the 75th anniversary of the park, which is located within 10 miles from the Harmony Motel.

After my U2 trip to Harmony Motel and Joshua Tree National Park, I had lunch at Elvis' favorite Palm Springs restaurant Las Casuelas. My friend Aaron from high school and his two friends, who were in Palm Springs for the weekend, met me there. We had great Mexican food and great conversation. It was a good time. I highly recommend the Enchiladas Rancheros. After lunch, I walked around downtown Palm Springs before returning to my wonderful A Place in the Sun garden hotel, where I spent a relaxing evening on my patio and eating great New York style delivery pizza.

Day 31 – June 13

The next morning we left fabulous Palm Springs around 10:15am and were in Anaheim by noon. It was 89 degrees when we left Palm Srings and 73 degrees when we arrived in Anaheim. What a difference 90 miles makes.

The hotels gods continued to shine on me in Anaheim. I checked into the TownePlace Suites to find the manager had upgraded me to a two bedroom suite. I was very happy because I was going to be there for six nights. It was much more comfortable having an apartment-like suite as opposed to a small hotel room. This was the longest I would stay at anyone place along my trip. I had three flatscreen tvs, two bedrooms, a living room with a couch and coffee table, a dining table, bathroom and a full kitchen. I was at the end of the hall on the first floor right by the door, which was really convenient for the dogs. It was like our own little apartment in Anaheim for six nights. Plus it was only a 10 minute walk to Angels Stadium for the U2 shows.

After unloading everything out of my car, I went to the grocery store, which was only a mile down the road. I got enough groceries to last the week as well as for my three-day drive across the county to Baltimore the following week. After grocery shopping, I did two loads of laundry because I had no clean clothes at all. Then I unpacked and organized the rest of my things and planned the rest of my week in Southern California.

Day 32 – June 14

The next morning StarLine tours picked me up at 9am at my hotel for their VIP tour of downtown LA, Hollywood, Beverly Hills, the original Farmer's Market, Venice Beach and Marina Del Ray. The first part of our bus trip, which was mostly folks from England and myself, took us to downtown Los Angeles.

Our first stop was the LA Memorial Coliseum, the site of the 1932 and 1984 Olympics and where the Dodgers used to play. We passed by USC on the way to the Staples Center and the Nokia Theatre. We drove through the financial district on our way to our next stop at Olvera Street, where there were streets vendors and LA's oldest house built in 1818. On our way to Hollywood, we drove by the Capitol Records building. Then across from the Hollywood Bowl, I spotted Bret Michael's tour bus parked with the shades closed. I found out that he was playing the Hollywood Bowl that night.

We finally made it to Hollywood Boulevard and had about 45 minutes to walk around. I walked down the Walk of Stars and saw Mickey Mouse at his star and then came upon Olivia Newton-John's star, which is the only thing I remembered from our family vacation back in 1984. I walked by the historic Roosevelt Hotel to check out the footprints at Grauman's Chinese Theatre. The first I saw were for the movie *Giant*, which consisted of the footprints of Rock Hudson and Elizabeth Taylor. It should have also included James Dean, but he died, so instead director George Steven's footprints were included. I came across the footprints of Natalie Wood, Bing Crosby, Paul Newman and Joanne Woodward together, Roy Rogers and Trigger, Dean Martin, Marilyn Monroe, Bette Davis, John Travolta, Nic Cage and finally Lana Turner. I searched everywhere for my favorite actress Lana Turner's footprints and finally had to ask someone.

I left the Chinese Theatre to find higher ground so I could see the Hollywood sign. On my way, I came across a lot of people camped out in line on Hollywood Boulevard. I asked why they were waiting out. As U2 fans had done in Denver and Seattle, these folks had also brought shoes to donate to Souls for Soul and were waiting for their free U2 tickets from the Hard Rock Cafe. I went into the Hard Rock to get my dad a pin, as he collects them, and was told that June 14, 2011 was the 40th anniversary of the Hard Rock. June 14th is also my parents' wedding anniversary. I finally made it up the Egyptian mall to see the Hollywood sign, but it was very hazy and far away, but at least I saw it though.

We got back on the bus and headed through West Hollywood on Sunset Boulevard, which is actually Route 66. We drove by the Chateau Marmont where John Belushi died and where Marilyn Monroe lived. We saw Mel's Drive In, where the movie *American Graffiti* was filmed. That parking lot looked much larger in the movie. We also drove by the Viper Room and saw the corner where River Phoenix died and drove by the Whiskey and the Roxy.

We then drove through Beverly Hills and saw the former homes of Marilyn Monroe, Frank Sinatra and Sammy Davis Jr. We drove down Rodeo Drive and saw the most expensive car ever, $2.2M, and we drove by the Beverly Wilshire hotel. Our next stop was lunch at the Farmer's Market, which was the first farmer's market in the US. I had lunch at Du-par's, which has been there since 1938. I noticed actress Diane Ladd was having lunch a few tables away. I snuck a picture, but it was too dark. The farmer's market is located next door to CBS Studios, so I stood by the gate for a bit to see if I could see my favorite Maura West leaving *Young and the Restless*, but I didn't see anyone.

Next we were off to the beaches. We drove on Santa Monica Boulevard, which is route 10 the longest freeway in the U.S. from the west coast to Jacksonville, Florida. We didn't stop in Santa Monica, but drove by the Santa Monica Pier. It was cloudy at the beach, but I could still see the pier – sort of. We then stopped at Venice Beach, and what a crazy place that was. It was a crowded cement boardwalk full of street vendors, dogs, bicycles, segweys, skateboarders and roller skaters. In a span of 45 minutes, I saw someone pass out and taken away by an ambulance, took part in a Lipton tea commercial, and smelled all sorts of marijuana. It was quite an eventful 45 minutes.

The last stop of our tour was at Fisherman's Village in Marina Del Ray, which is the largest man-made marina in the world. It was nice to smell the salt air again. I had the best strawberry milkshake there. I really enjoyed my day touring around LA and was glad I took the bus tour because it made it stress free, but it was sort of a blur. I was so concerned with getting all the pictures and videos of every hot spot in the time allotted at each place.

Days 33 – June 15

I didn't sleep at all the night after my great tour of LA, so I decided to just stay in bed all day. I watched *Country Strong* on pay per view and napped. That night I had dinner with my cousin Cherie and her husband Mike, who only lived a few miles from my hotel. After our yummy Mexican dinner at Fresca's, we went back to their house and hung out with their dogs.

Day 34 – June 16

They refer to the weather in June in Southern California as 'June Gloom' and it certainly was. It was cloudy, cool and humid. I didn't think California had humidity. It was 68 degrees with 70% humidity. In the morning I took Big Orange, my Saturn, to Hardin GMC for an oil change and make sure everything was ok for my long 3000 mile drive across the country in a few days.

In the afternoon, I went to Downtown Disney, which was basically an outside mall with lots of shops and restaurants including ESPNZone and House of Blues. I wanted to check it out since I was in Anaheim a few miles from Disneyland, but had no interest in actually going to

Disneyland. There would be too many kids, plus I didn't want to ride the rides. So I walked around Downtown Disney and had lunch on the patio at La Brea Bakery Cafe. I had a great caesar salad and cheese sliders. For once I didn't get a tuna melt. After lunch I went into the huge World of Disney store and bought some souvenirs. I told myself I wouldn't buy any tee shirts this summer while traveling across the U.S., but thus far I had bought four – one from Red Rocks, a Nirvana tee from Seattle, one from Joshua Tree and one from Disney.

U2 show #64 – June 17, 2011 – Anaheim

Day 35 of my U2 360 Tour Across America brought me to Angels Stadium for the first of two 360 shows. It had been 10 days since the last U2 show. These next two shows in Anaheim were going to be fantastic. The second was to be my favorite of the tour. That first Anaheim show had a much better energy than the first five 360 shows I had seen. The audience was really into it, but it was the same set list as the previous U.S. shows I had seen.

I spent the day in my hotel room conserving my energy as I did on every show day. I left for Angels Stadium at 2pm. I got a little lost walking to the stadium – I went the wrong way twice. I got to the stadium shortly after 2:30, even though the stadium is just a few blocks from my hotel. I was tired and sweaty, as June Gloom brought the humidity in Southern California. I think I got a little overheated and dehydrated because I had a terrible migraine the rest of the day and throughout the show.

Arriving at the stadium on June 17th, I noticed there were two GA lines on opposite sides of the stadium. I walked around to where I thought the band would drive in and found most of my friends already there waiting. I hung out with Chuck and Michelle, whom I had met in Seattle. I also met Tesh and Danielle. We were in the wrong place, so we moved around to the right place about a half hour later. U2 arrived around 4pm, not in their usual black town cars, but all in one white van. They had flown in on helicopters and landed across the way and then drove over to the stadium. No one stopped, but Larry did smile as he drove by. I like to think it was because he saw my "Larry Mullen Band" shirt. This was the first time Bono did not stop in the U.S. on that leg.

We got in the GA line and listened to the sound check, which included both "The Fly" and "Ultra Violet," but neither were played in the show. We entered the stadium just after 5pm, got our neck stamped to re-enter the inner circle and then went up to the stands to sit and relax in the shade. Anaheim Stadium is a beautiful baseball park – the prettiest of all the stadiums I've seen.

Lenny Kravitz and his band arrived to the stage in golf carts. They played from 7:30 to about 8:15 and the same set list as the previous four shows I had seen. After Lenny's performance, I went back behind the stage to wait for U2 to walk in. The venue security tried to get us to leave, but Rocco, U2's stage manager, told them we were allowed to stay there to wait for the band. U2 walked to the stage just after 9pm and Larry once again smiled and waved at me as he entered.

The inner circle was very crowded, probably because of all the VIPs. I stayed behind the stage for the entire show, which is fine because that's the best view of Larry anyway. Plus I was nauseated from my migraine that I needed to lean against the railing. During "Even Better Than the Real Thing," Bono said, "End of the June Gloom" referring to the month of humidity and clouds in Southern California. He went on to say, "Angels, where you gonna take us tonight?" referring to the Anaheim Angels baseball team. During "Magnificent," Bono again referred to Arch Bishop TuTu as "our boss the Arch," but then went on to say, "our other boss The Edge."

I completely misunderstood the band introductions at the time. It wasn't until I listened to the bootleg of the show that I understood what Bono had meant. I thought Bono was talking about Larry, but he was talking about Paul McGuinness. Bono said, "Tonight might be the night to toast a man who's meant so much to this band. A man to whom we owe so much. A man without whom I don't think we would be here tonight. Without this man, things might have turned out a little differently. Larry Mullen Jr (long pause) would not be a drummer in U2. He'd be a highway patrolman, but in Dublin." I was screaming so loudly that I didn't hear the rest of the band introductions. After saying what he, Edge and Adam would be if not in U2, Bono toasted Paul whose 60th birthday was the day before. And for the first time ever, Paul McGuinness was brought on stage and we sang "Happy Birthday" to him.

Bono dedicated "Pride" to Maria Shriver, who was in the audience. Before "Vertigo," Bono said, "Big love across the border Mexico ... Viva Mexico!" During "I'll Go Crazy if I Don't Go Crazy Tonight," Bono said, "How crazy can it get in Anaheim?" After "Walk On," Bono again said, "End of the June Gloom Anaheim." During "With or Without You," I went back to wait for U2 to leave. I stood in the same place I did in Seattle (near the tunnel), hoping that Larry would once again grace me with a handshake. Before "Moment of Surrender," Bono said, "We've never had a bad time in this neighborhood." Larry didn't come over to shake my hand, but he did smile and wave at me. So a smile and wave from Larry on the way into the show and on the way out of the show isn't too shabby.

The set list for the first 360 show in Anaheim on June 17, 2011 was as follows: Even Better Than The Real Thing, I Will Follow, Get On Your Boots, Magnificent, The Great Curve / Mysterious Ways, Elevation, Until the End of the World,

Happy Birthday, All I Want Is You, Stay / In the Wee Small Hours of the Morning, Beautiful Day / Space Oddity, Pride, Miss Sarajevo, Zooropa, City of Blinding Lights, Vertigo / Are You Gonna Go My Way, I'll Go Crazy / Discotheque / Life During Wartime / Psycho Killer, Sunday Bloody Sunday, Scarlet, Walk On / You'll Never Walk Alone, One / United We Stand, Will You Love Me Tomorrow / Where the Streets Have No Name, Hold Me Thrill Me Kiss Me Kill Me, With or Without You, Moment of Surrender.

U2 show #65 – June 18, 2011 – Anaheim

The next morning on Day 36 of my U2 360 Tour Across America, I woke up and did it all over again. Anaheim was the only city where U2 played two back to back shows on that final leg of the 360 tour. I almost didn't go to the second show because it was on a Saturday night, and I had to drive across the country in three days to make it to the show in Baltimore on Wednesday night. People were trying to get me to skip the show to make the drive easier, but I decided to stay. And thank goodness I did because Anaheim2 was my favorite show of the U2 360 tour.

I again stayed in my hotel room all day until I left for Angels stadium at 2:30. I didn't get lost that second day, so I arrived very quickly. I got my GA wristband and went to wait for U2 to arrive. They again arrived in 2 helicopters, a white van and again did not stop. I went inside after the GA line had already gone in. It was a more relaxed feel than the previous night. The inner circle wasn't as crowded. I again got a soda and sat in the stands until Lenny Kravitz came on. As I walked around the general admission area, I saw Cindy Crawford. She was stunning and very nice – posing for pictures. I saw my friends Chuck, Matt, Melissa and Kim. I went behind the stage and stood at the tunnel where U2 would walk into the stadium. I again watched the show from behind the stage, so I could watch Larry – as I did almost every show of the tour.

That second night in Anaheim on June 18th, U2 finally changed the set list – and change it they did! With every new change, I grew more and more excited! For the first and only time in the U.S., U2 started the show with five straight songs from "Achtung Baby," celebrating its 20th anniversary. During "Even Better Than the Real Thing," Bono said, "Southern California. Orange County. Where you gonna take us tonight? You take us higher!" And that they did. The second song of the night was "The Fly," which hadn't been played since 2006 in Hawaii, but would remain in the set list for the rest of the tour. During "The Fly," Bono yelled, "Achtung Ya'll!" just as he had during ZooTv. This got me SO excited! "Where the Streets Have No Name," which is usually in the encore, was the 6th song of the night, following "Until the End of the World" and "One."

During "Get on Your Boots" right before my favorite "LET ME IN THE SOUND!", Bono said, "Larry Mullen do you know how beautiful you are?" Bono introduced Larry as "a movie star" saying, "it had to happen." He went on to say, "our Lawrence plays opposite the great Donald Sutherland in *The Man on the Train*." My favorite part of the night was when U2 finally brought my favorite song "I Still Haven't Found What I'm Looking For" back into the set list for the first time that leg – and it remained there for the rest of the tour. Bono dedicated it to Quincy Jones, who was in the audience, and said, "This song means a great deal to us." I cried like a baby, literally tears streaming down my face. This was one of my favorite moments of the entire 360 tour – very special to me. I'll never forget it!

U2 played "Stuck in a Moment" instead of "Stay," which made me extremely happy. Bono of course dedicated it to Michael Hutchence, but also talked about Edge and how he would be a great neighbor – referring to the petition against him building a house there. Bono also mentioned that it was Edge's wedding anniversary. The black lighted jackets made a return during "Zooropa" and "City of Blinding Lights." I loved Larry in that black leather jacket! Larry smiled at me during "I'll Go Crazy."

There was only one encore at that second show in Anaheim. A sixth song from *Achtung Baby,* "Ultra Violet," made its way into the set list for the first time that leg replacing "Hold Me Thrill Me Kiss Me Kill Me." The rest of the two U2 would pretty much alternate these two songs. Before "Moment of Surrender," Bono sang a part of "Jungleland" paying tribute to Clarence Clemons who died earlier that day. He would do this for the remainder of the tour. "Magnificent" was left out of the set list for the first and only time that leg. I again went back near the tunnel to watch U2 leave the stadium. Larry saw me and smiled and waved and seemed like he wanted to come over, but didn't – but he kept looking back at me.

The set list for my favorite show of the U2 360 tour, Anaheim2 on June 18, 2011, was as follows: Even Better Than The Real Thing, The Fly, Mysterious Ways / Don't Speak, Until the End of the World, One, Amazing Grace / Where the Streets Have No Name / All You Need Is Love, I Will Follow, Get On Your Boots / She Loves You, ***I Still Haven't Found What I'm Looking For***, Stuck In a Moment, Beautiful Day / Space Oddity, Elevation, Pride, Miss Sarajevo, Zooropa, City of Blinding Lights, Vertigo / It's Only Rock and Roll, I'll Go Crazy / Discotheque / Please, Sunday Bloody Sunday, Scarlet, Walk On / Never Walk Alone, Ultraviolet, With or Without You, Moment of Surrender / Jungleland.

I had the best time at that second show in Anaheim! I am SO glad I didn't skip it just to get a head start on my cross country drive to Baltimore. Never listen to reason. Follow your passion. That show ended part two of my U2 360 road trip. The main sightseeing part of my trip was over. That first month was my favorite part of my trip, even though it only contained one of my favorite shows because traveling out west was my favorite.

On the Road to Baltimore

Day 37 – June 19

On Sunday, the morning after the second U2 show in Anaheim, I left for my cross country trip to Baltimore. I had just three and a half days to drive 2700 miles from California to Maryland to make it to the U2 show in Baltimore on Wednesday. It was very important that I go to the Baltimore show because it is my hometown show, and I have great memories from the Elevation show in Baltimore 10 years prior.

People tried to dissuade me from trying to make that long journey in just three and half days, but I've never really listened to reason. Some said I should either skip the second Anaheim show or skip the Baltimore show in order to have a more relaxing drive. I didn't want to skip either. I had made the challenge to myself to drive to every U2 show in the U.S. on that final leg of the 360 tour, so I had to try. For those three and a half days, I survived on subway subs, cheese crackers, pizza, water and sweet tea, stopping at Love's and spending nights at Motel 6s along the way.

That first day Elvis, Cilla and I drove 777 miles from Anaheim to Albuquerque in 12 hours, stopping just three times. I passed through the towns in Arizona and New Mexico along Route 66 that I didn't get to see the previous year on my Route 66 road trip from Tulsa to Albuquerque.

Day 38 – June 20

The next morning we left Albuquerque at 6:15am, drove 733 miles to Ft. Smith, Arkansas in 11 hours, stopping just twice. It was 104 degrees in Clinton, Oklahoma and so windy that it literally blew the dogs over. I had wanted to make it to Little Rock or even Memphis, but I just couldn't do it. I was wiped. It was the first day of my trip I did not enjoy the drive, although I did enjoy passing by Cadillac Ranch and the Big Texan ranch in Amarillo, Texas where I had so much fun the previous year.

Day 39 – June 21

On the third day of our drive we left Ft. Smith at 5:40am, drove 863 miles in 14 hours to Wytheville, Virginia, stopping four times including my house in Memphis. We sat in traffic and drove through blinding rain storms. It was another day of terrible driving.

U2 show #66 – June 22, 2011 – Baltimore

The next morning, Day 40 of my U2 360 Tour Across America, we left Wytheville, Virginia at 6:10am, drove 326 miles and arrived at my parents' house in Ellicott City, Maryland at 11:25am, stopping twice along the way. I finally made it! I left Anaheim, California at 7:30am pacific time Sunday June 19th and 2700 miles and three days later arrived in Ellicott City, Maryland the morning of the U2 360 show in Baltimore, the reward for my for my crazy cross country mad dash. Tasha arrived at my parents' house around 1, and we headed to downtown Baltimore about 20 minutes away. I was born and raised in Baltimore, so this U2 360 show in Baltimore was my hometown show. It was my 66th U2 show and my 7th of this leg of the 360 tour. It was the 10th anniversary of the last show on the 1st leg of Elevation (6.22.01). It was 10 years ago in Baltimore on the Elevation tour when Larry hugged me. Before it even started, this U2 360 show in Baltimore was special to me.

When we arrived at Ravens Stadium, we walked around the stadium to see where U2 would arrive, sat under a tree and waited. It was so hot that day in Baltimore. It proved to be one of the hottest shows of the tour, even hotter than Miami. U2 drove in a couple hours after we arrived, but again they did not stop. I was really disappointed because I thought they would definitely stop in Baltimore like that had 10 years prior, plus they hadn't stopped before either show in Anaheim. We got into the inner circle, and it wasn't crowded yet. We would have had a great view, but we decided to walk around. We ran into our friends at the soundboard and watched Florence and the Machine from there. She was good, but a little too screamy for me. I definitely preferred Lenny Kravitz.

As I did every show, I went behind the stage to wait for U2 to enter the stadium. This time they came out of the tunnel on Adam's side, but still walked onto the stage on Edge's side where I was. As Larry walked by, he smile and waved at me like usual but the look in his eyes was one of surprise that seemed to say, 'You're here too? Didn't I just see you in Anaheim?' He kept looking at me. Then I was jolted out of my Larry bliss by a severe pain in my arm. A woman I had just met was standing next to me and was SO excited to see Bono walk by that she pinched my arm so hard that it hurt for the first three songs – and bruised for three days!

During "Even Better Than the Real Thing," I ran over to Adam's side of the inner circle to watch the show with Tasha because she loves Adam. But I ended up watching the show behind the stage so I could watch Larry. Before the band introductions, Bono commented about how hot it was in Baltimore and how beautiful "MARY-land" is. He said it reminded him of Wicklow in Ireland. When introducing the band, Bono said, "Larry has become a movie star. It had to happen." Then he joked and said Larry was going to star as Billy Idol in an HBO biopic. On this rare occasion Bono said, "Lawrence Mullen on the drums" rather than Larry Mullen. Bono dedicated "Pride" to Eunice Shriver and at the end got choked up when the audience continued to sing. I'm really not sure why fans are so tired of hearing "Pride" live? At the beginning of "I'll Go Crazy If I Don't Go Crazy Tonight," Larry started walking toward the back and Sammy had to catch up with him to give him his conga. Larry looked down at me and smiled. Then I ran around to the other bridge on Adam's side to wait for Larry to make his way back to the stage. He smiled at me as he ran by before he threw his conga to Sammy.

At the end of the show, I wanted to watch U2 leave thinking maybe Larry would come over to me like he did in Seattle. We could see their cars parked in the tunnel – they were so close they were almost inside the stadium. When they left the stage, U2 walked straight to their cars, they didn't even look over to us. But I kept watching Larry. He was almost at his car when he tore off his shirt, and I saw his naked back! Then he put on a black robe. That was almost as good as a handshake. We watched the cars pull away and stood there soaking (and screaming) in the moment. Then someone from the crew came over to me and gave me the set list. Maybe it was all the screaming, and he wanted to calm me down.

The set list for Baltimore was similar to Anaheim2. Both shows were used sort of used as a rehearsal for the

Glastonbury Festival that followed. "Magnificent" was still not played, while "The Fly" and "I Still Haven't Found What I'm Looking For" remained. "One" and "Where the Streets Have No Name" were moved back to their regular spots in the set list. U2 had played "40" during the sound check, but not in the actual show. The Baltimore audience went nuts for "Beautiful Day" and again for "Streets." They really sang along with "I Still Haven't Found What I'm Looking For" and "Pride," proving my point that these two songs should never be left off the set list. The Baltimore crowd surprised me with their enthusiasm. It was the loudest crowd I heard the entire 360 tour. Those Ravens fans are loud!

The set list for the U2 360 show in Baltimore on June 22, 2011 was as follows: Even Better Than The Real Thing, The Fly, Mysterious Ways, Until the End of the World, I Will Follow, Get On Your Boots, I Still Haven't Found What I'm Looking For / The Promised Land, Stay / In The Wee Small Hours Of The Morning, Beautiful Day / Space Oddity, Elevation, Pride, Miss Sarajevo, Zooropa, City of Blinding Lights, Vertigo, I'll Go Crazy / Discotheque / Life During Wartime / Psycho Killer, Sunday Bloody Sunday, Scarlet, Walk On / You'll Never Walk Alone, One, Amazing Grace / Where the Streets Have No Name / All You Need Is Love, Ultraviolet, With or Without You, Moment of Surrender / Jungleland.

Elvis, Cilla and I spent the next two days after the Baltimore show relaxing at my parents' house in Ellicott City, Maryland eating Ledo's pizza before heading up to Michigan for next U2 show in East Lansing.

On the Road to East Lansing

Day 43 – June 25

Three days after the U2 show in Baltimore, I left my parents' house in Ellicott City, Maryland at 10am and arrived in East Lansing, Michigan at 7:30pm – driving 578 miles stopping only twice. It was a long, boring drive along the Pennsylvania and Ohio turnpikes, costing me a total of $22. in tolls. Over the next month, I would drive back and forth across the Pennsylvania and Ohio Turnpikes over and over again.

They were very excited in East Lansing for the U2 360 show at Michigan State University. There was a U2 flyer and a newspaper with U2 on the cover at the front desk of my hotel, the Howard Johnson. Apparently U2 hadn't played in East Lansing since the early 1980s and there hasn't been a stadium concert there since the Rolling Stones in the early 1990s. I had never been to Michigan before, and unfortunately I didn't have time to do any sightseeing on this trip. I just had just enough time to drive up from Maryland, see the U2 show, and then drive down to Miami for the next U2 show. Maybe next time U2 could have a more logical geographic tour for those of us crazy fans following them.

U2 show #67 – June 26, 2011 – East Lansing, MI

Day 44 of my U2 360 Tour Across America was the halfway point. The U2 360 show at Michigan State in East Lansing was good. It was same set list as the Baltimore show, except "Hold Me Thrill Me Kiss Me Kill Me" was played instead of "Ultra Violet." It stayed light outside
through "Elevation," which was really cool because I have never seen a U2 show in the daylight before. This East

Lansing show was the least crowded 360 show I went to, even though it was sold out. They didn't sell many GA tickets, so there was plenty of room inside the inner circle and the rest of the floor wasn't even half full. There were no red zones and the catwalk of the inner circle went almost to the stands.

    I started off my day in Michigan relaxing in my hotel room, ordered a pizza and walked to Spartan Stadium, which was only about a mile away, around 1:30 pm. I walked around the stadium to the GA line, which seemed very calm and happy. The GA line was right by the entrance the crew was using to go in and out of the stadium, so everyone assumed U2 would be arriving there – but it was at the opposite end of the stage. I walked around the stadium to see if there was anywhere else U2 could drive in. When I returned to where I started, Dallas and Sammy were also walking back. I asked Sammy if U2 were really arriving here in front of the GA line, and he said there was no else they could come in. Then Dallas asked how I was doing and shook my hand. A little while later Rocco informed us that U2 was not doing a sound check, so this indicated to me that U2 was going to arrive very late.

    I decided to go back over to where the catering was set up and where the crew was going in and out of. There was no back stage in the stadium and no dressing rooms. They had set up a 'backstage' at the hockey arena around the corner. I waited there, later joined by Beth and Tim. Even though I had met Beth in Denver, I didn't really hang out with her or get to know her that day in East Lansing. We stayed until almost 8pm and nothing. We saw Florence and the Machine arrive and leave, but no U2. We learned later that U2 was driven right up to the stadium and let out there. This was the first time on this leg of the tour that I had not seen U2 arrive at the stadium, unfortunately it wouldn't be my last. This was also the fourth show in a row Bono did not stop and greet the fans before the show as he did for the first four shows of that final leg of 360.

I went into Spartan Stadium at 8pm and still got inside the inner circle and up to the stage. There was so much room and behind the stage was smaller, narrower. We didn't have wristbands and were not allowed to go up into the stands for concessions or bathrooms. There were no red zones. I stayed on Adam's side of the stage because I realized U2 were again going to enter on Adam's side. This was the first time I was not on Edge's side of the stage to see them walk under the stage. U2 actually entered through the stands – walking down the bleachers through the fans. U2 started their walk to the stage just after 8:45, and it was still light out and stayed light until 9:40 through "Elevation." It was definitely a much different experience watching a U2 show in the daylight. East Lansing is still eastern standard time, but right on the border. Just a few miles west and it would have been 7:45.

I watched the first part of the show from Adam's side of the stage and could even see Edge. It was nice to have a good view without being squished. I like to be behind the stage, so I can watch Larry, but I also like having a lot of room around me. During "Even Better Than the Real Thing," Bono said, "Go green. Go white. Go orange. Where are you going to take the Irish tonight? You take us higher." I was very excited when Bono said, "Achtung Y'all!" during "The Fly" like he used to on ZooTv. He said it in Anaheim2 and Baltimore, but he seemed to really scream it in East Lansing. During the time Bono usually introduces the band, he said they were very happy to be at MSU and how U2 never made it to university. Bono went on to say, "U2 became our university. Rolling Stone became our text books. We're still students. I Still Haven't Found What I'm Looking For." Now that is how you introduce a song!

The video screens were black for the Mark Kelly intro to "Beautiful Day," but then came back on during the song. Bono did quick band introductions during "Elevation" saying "Larry Mullen is a prince of a man." During "Mysterious Ways," Larry's drum kit turned around so I went behind the stage. He saw me and gave me a big smile! I went back to up to the side of the stage until the end of the "Pride" when I went back behind the stage and stayed there until Larry started "I'll Go Crazy If I Don't Go Crazy Tonight." I got my usual nod and smile from Larry. Then I moved around to wait for Larry to make his way around the catwalk and watch him trot over the bridge and throw his conga to Sammy. It was great East Lansing was not so crowded so I could stalk, I mean follow, Larry around during the show.

The set list for the 360 show in East Lansing on June 26, 2011 was as follows: Even Better Than The Real Thing, The Fly, Mysterious Ways, Until the End of the World, I Will Follow, Get On Your Boots, I Still Haven't Found What I'm Looking For / The Promised Land, Stay, Beautiful Day – Space Oddity, Elevation, Pride, Miss Sarajevo, Zooropa, City of Blinding Lights, Vertigo / T.V. Eye, I'll Go Crazy / Discotheque / Psycho Killer / Life During Wartime, Sunday Bloody Sunday, Scarlet, Walk On / You'll Never Walk Alone, One, Will You Love Me Tomorrow / Where the Streets Have No Name, Hold Me Thrill Me Kiss Me Kill Me, With or Without You, Moment of Surrender / Jungleland.

On the Road to Miami

Day 45 & 46 – June 27 & 28

In two days, I drove 1,426 miles from East Lansing, Michigan to Miami, Florida bringing my miles driven over

10,500 miles and still had eight more shows to go. I left Michigan the morning after the U2 show, drove through Dayton and Cincinatti, Ohio, drove through the blinding rain in Kentucky (Elvis' "Kentucky Rain" comes to mind), and stayed the night at a Motel 6 in Chattanooga, Tennessee. The next morning we left Chattanooga, got stuck in the horrible Atlanta traffic, drove through Macon, Georgia, drove through the blinding rain in Florida as U2's "Summer Rain" coincidently played on my ipod, and finally arrived at the lovely Epic Hotel in Miami at 8:00pm. After two long days of driving, it was wonderful to relax in such a luxurious hotel!

The Resort Manager at the Epic heard about my U2 360 tour across America and graciously upgraded me to a fabulous suite with separate living room, bedroom, huge bathroom, and a wrap around balcony with doors off the living room and bedroom. I could have lived there! Because she knew I had a long drive from Michigan and would be arriving late, the manager had a cheese plate and chilled white wine waiting for me – and this amazing, huge chocolate U2 guitar! There were also framed pictures of my Elvis and Cilla and U2. Kimpton Hotels know how to do customer service!

Because this suite was so fabulously relaxing, I decided to stay the day after the U2 show and make the drive to Nashville in one day rather than diving it up over two days. I would come to regret that decision because I didn't realize it was the Friday of the 4th of July holiday weekend and traffic was horrible, especially through Atlanta. But at the time I just wanted to stay in one place for more than a day – and it was such a fabulous hotel.

U2 show #68 – June 29, 2011 – Miami

The U2 360 show in Miami was great! It was the same set list as East Lansing except U2 played "North Star" for the first time in the U.S. I had a great Larry moment during "I'll Go Crazy." It was hot in Miami, but not as hot as it was at the Baltimore show.

I spent the first half of Day 47 of my U2 360 Tour Across America relaxing in my fabulous suite at the wonderful Epic hotel. I left the hotel at 2:00 and was parked at Sun Life Stadium about 10 miles away by 3pm. Luckily I didn't have to walk too far to find out where everyone was waiting for U2 to arrive. Around 5:30 U2 finally arrived, but again did not stop. I guess since they stopped and greeted the fans the first four shows I went to, I just assumed they would stop every time. I shouldn't have taken it for granted when I spoke with Bono in Seattle and Oakland.

There was still a GA line at when I was ready to go in at 6pm, so I had to wait in line. I got into the inner circle with my 'Happy Birthday' re-entry stamp. I stayed on Edge's side of the inner circle so I could watch U2 enter under the stage. While waiting, I hung out with Rick, as was becoming a habit on 360. I talked with my new friend Patty whom I would see again in Pittsburgh. The inner circle was pretty full by 7pm. Florence and the Machine didn't start until 7:45. Florence ran into the stadium in her bare feet with her arms spread out as if she was flying down the walkway out of the tunnel and onto the stage.

U2 didn't come on until 9:15. During "Even Better Than the Real Thing," Bono shouted, "Miami! My Mammy!" just like Popmart. Bono again shouted "Achtung Y'all!" during "The Fly" and introduced it 'circa 1991.' It has taken me 20 years, but "The Fly" has become one of my favorite songs live.

During the band introductions, Bono talked about the many stadiums of Miami: Joe Robbie, Pro Player, Sun Life. He said they had played them all. I'm not sure if he realized they were all the same stadiums – just with different names over the years. Bono went on to say that U2 had played some of their best shows in Miami and had opened ZooTv there, but he didn't mention opening and closing the Elevation tour in Miami. Bono talked about how Irish people can't dance. He said, "Larry Mullen, he doesn't even try to dance."

U2 debuted "North Star" in the U.S., in the place where "Stay" or "Stuck in a Moment" is usually played. After, Bono said maybe they should have rehearsed it a little. I thought it sounded fine. During "I'll Go Crazy If I Don't Go Crazy Tonight," Larry looked at me, smiled and mouthed something to me. I'm not sure what it was, maybe 'Hi' or 'Thanks', but we locked eyes for a few moments. At the end of "I'll Go Crazy," Bono again said, "Miami. My Mammy." U2 exited on Adam's side, even though they had entered on Edge's side, but Larry did look in my direction as he came down the stairs from the stage. The Miami audience as a whole was enthusiastic and loud, but the folks around me in the inner circle didn't seem too excited. It took me over two hours to get out of the parking lot at Sun Life Stadium, so I didn't get back to the hotel until almost 2am. Luckily I was staying put the next day, rather than starting my trip to Nashville in the morning. This was one of only three times I drove to a show on that last leg of the 360 Tour.

The set list for the 360 show in Miami on June 29, 2011 was as follows: Even Better Than The Real Thing, The Fly, Mysterious Ways, Until the End of the World, I Will Follow, Get On Your Boots, I Still Haven't Found What I'm Looking For / The Promised Land, North Star, Beautiful Day / Space Oddity, Elevation, Pride, Miss Sarajevo, Zooropa, City of Blinding Lights, Vertigo, I'll Go Crazy), Sunday Bloody Sunday, Scarlet,

Walk On, One, Will You Love Me Tomorrow / Where the Streets Have No Name, Hold Me Thrill Me Kiss Me Kill Me, With or Without You, Moment of Surrender.

On the Road to Nashville

Day 49 – July 1

After the U2 show in Miami Wednesday night, I spent Thursday relaxing in my luxurious suite in the lovely Epic hotel. I left Miami at 6am est Friday morning and should have arrived in Nashville around 7pm cst. But because of horrible traffic around Atlanta, I didn't make it to Nashville until 9pm. I was in the car 16 hours driving over 925 miles. I was exhausted. Elvis and Cilla were exhausted. By the time I got checked in at the Hotel Indigo, unpacked and walked the dogs, it was after 10pm. I should have known better than to try to make it from Miami to Nashville in one day, especially when that one day was the Friday of the 4th of July weekend.

U2 show #69 – July 2, 2011 – Nashville

The U2 360 show in Nashville was fantastic, which was a nice reward for that long trafficy 16-hour drive from Miami the day before. It was my 50th day on my U2 360 Tour Across America, my 10th show that leg of the tour, my 69th U2 show overall and the 100th show of the entire 360 tour. I had been really looking forward to the Nashville show not only because it was sort of my hometown show (three hours from Memphis where I lived at the time), but also because U2 hadn't played in Nashville since 1981. I wasn't disappointed. There were some great moments at that U2 360 show in Nashville. U2 played "The Wanderer" for the first time, honoring Johnny Cash. And after "Moment of Surrender" as Larry, Edge and Adam started to walk off stage, Bono pulled a blind guy up on stage who played guitar while the band came back and played "All I Want is You" and then Bono gave him his green "goal is soul" guitar. What a moment!

My friend Tasha flew in early the morning of the U2 show in Nashville. We relaxed in our hotel room a bit, then had lunch at Blackstone on the way to Vanderbilt Stadium, which was about a seven block walk. We arrived at the stadium and talked with old U2 friends and met new ones. We immediately discovered where the band was going to enter – we saw the signs for the dressing rooms on the building attached to the stadium. Since it was hot and sunny, we decided to stand in the parking garage to wait for them. We had a great view of where U2 would get out of their cars and enter the building, or if they walked out to sign autographs and take pictures we could run down to meet them. Since it was a college stadium, there were dressing rooms inside the stadium. They had makeshift dressing rooms in the building next to the stadium.

After a couple hours, everyone else figured out where we were and joined in behind us. Edge arrived first, waited in the car a while, and then went into the building. We noticed that Edge's car had a Shelby County license plate, which is Memphis. Then we saw Willie Williams give Edge's security guy a Sun Studio tee shirt. Had U2 been in Memphis visiting Sun Studio and Graceland without me? Bono arrived next and started to walk toward us, but Brian pulled him back saying they didn't have time. Adam and Larry arrived at the same time. Adam got out of the car first and went into the building. Larry then got out of his car and smiled and waved to the fans then went into the building. I didn't get to speak to Larry, but this was the first time this tour I saw him arrive at the stadium and get out of his car and wave to us – because he had no choice, usually they are able to drive into the stadium.

We easily made it into the inner circle, even though it was a small college stadium. This was the last show Florence and the Machine opened, which was fine with me. I watched the show in Nashville from Adam's side of the stage because Tasha loves Adam. Also, U2 entered from Adam's side of the stage, so for only the second time I didn't watch U2 walk under the stage from Edge's side.

During "Even Better Than the Real Thing," Bono said, "In a sea of songs, where you going to take us tonight Music City?" Before "The Fly," Bono said, "Nashville, Tennessee! With love from Berlin 1991 'The Fly'," and then again in the middle shouted "Achtung Y'all!" Bono pulled our friend Dan up on stage during "I Will Follow" – it was Dan's birthday. There was a lot of echo during "I Will Follow," which I don't remember before.

During the band introductions, Bono mentioned U2 hadn't played Nashville since 1981 and then said his name is Bono and they are a 'band from Dublin, Ireland.' Bono went on to say, "Behind me the man who gave us our first job and made us as a result unemployable for anything else. He's a handsome man. He's a thoughtful man. And he's had that haircut since 1981. Larry Mullen on the drums." Before "I Still Haven't Found What I'm Looking For," Bono said, "In a city of masters, we're students. We'll stay students." Later in the song, Bono said their friend Cowboy Jack Clement was in the audience. Clement worked with Sam Phillips at Sun Studio in Memphis and recorded Elvis Presley, Johnny Cash, Jerry Lee Lewis and many others. Clement recorded U2 at Sun Studio for *Rattle and Hum*. Immediately following "Still Haven't Found," Bono started singing "The Wanderer" trying to imitate Johnny Cash's voice. At the end, he said, "forgive us Johnny." This was the first time "The Wanderer" had ever been played at a U2 concert. I heard the audience cheer for the first time when Bono sang, 'a shout rings out in the MEMPHIS sky' during "Pride."

After "Moment of Surrender," Edge, Larry and Adam were walking off stage when Bono announced they had a special guest. A guy appeared on stage and played guitar to "All I Want is You" while the rest of the band joined in. He dedicated the song to his wife and then Bono gave him his green 'Goal is Soul' guitar. Never leave a U2 show early. Security was really annoying and wouldn't let us stand to watch U2 walk out of the stadium, but we managed anyway. After screaming LARRY a few times, he finally turned to me and smiled and waved. As we were walking out of the stadium, we noticed the fan who was on stage playing "All I Want is You" was walking out right in front of us. He was blind, and he didn't have the guitar with him. He said he had a sign saying something like 'pull a blind man up on stage' and they were mailing him the guitar. He also said he didn't realize what was going on. He thought the concert was over and then Bono pulled him up on stage. I later realized he was the same guy who had been emailing me earlier that day looking for a GA ticket. #SmallWorld

The set list for the Nashville 360 show on July 2, 2011 was as follows: Even Better Than The Real Thing, The Fly, Mysterious Ways, Until the End of the World, I Will Follow, Get On Your Boots, I Still Haven't Found What I'm Looking For / The Wanderer, Stay, Beautiful Day / Space Oddity, Elevation, Pride, Miss Sarajevo, Zooropa, City of Blinding Lights, Vertigo, I'll Go Crazy / Discotheque / Psycho Killer / Life During Wartime, Sunday Bloody Sunday, Scarlet, Walk On – You'll Never Walk Alone, One, Amazing Grace / Where the Streets Have No Name, Hold Me Thrill Me Kiss Me Kill Me, With or Without You, Moment of Surrender, All I Want Is You.

On the Road to Chicago

Day 51 – July 3

The morning after the U2 show in Nashville, we drove to Hendersonville about a half hour away to visit Johnny Cash's grave. Tasha and I are both big Johnny Cash fans and had never been to his grave, even though I had lived in Memphis the past three years. We would have visited his house too, but it burned down a few years prior. After Hendersonville, we passed by the Corvette museum in Bowling Green, Kentucky and stopped at Abraham Lincoln's birthplace in Kentucky before we made our way to Chicago.

Day 52 – July 4

My friends Tasha and Amy and I spent the 4th of July in Chicago walking up and down Michigan Avenue. We ran into some of our U2 friends, had lunch at the Purple Pig and hung out in Millenium Park before relaxing in our room at the Hotel Monaco, another great Kimpton hotel. We had thought about going to the White Sox game, but decided against it. We should have gone because we found out later that Larry was there with the U2 360 crew. I can only imagine Larry's face had I sat down next to him in the stands at the baseball game. #RestrainingOrder

U2 show #70 – July 5, 2011 – Chicago

The U2 360 show in Chicago was amazing!!!! U2 played "Out of Control," which had not been played in the U.S. on the 360 tour! I like it so much better than "I Will Follow." It has a better energy, so much more exciting. I had been wanting them to play it all tour. The shock of the night was when U2 closed the show with the spur of the moment addition of "One Tree Hill," which they had not played in the U.S. since 1987! I love "One Tree Hill" as it is off my favorite album *The Joshua Tree*. We met The Edge before the show and saw John Cusack watching the show. A great, great show – my favorite U2 360 show, along with Anaheim2. Soldier Field was the only venue where I saw U2 on two different legs of the 360 tour.

    The day of U2 show in Chicago, Day 53 of my U2 360 Tour Across America, Tasha and I relaxed in the hotel all morning and early afternoon. We had lunch in the hotel restaurant before going to Soldier Field. Since it was 2 miles from our hotel, we took a cab because we didn't want to pay $46 for parking or get stuck in traffic after. We arrived at the stadium around 2:30 and waited for U2 to arrive. We knew exactly where to wait because we were at Soldier Field in 2009 for the U2 360 opener of the U.S. tour.

    Around 5:30, U2 arrived at Soldier Field. I'm not sure who arrived first because we couldn't see who was in what car, except we did see Edge and Bono drive in. A few minutes later, Edge walked back out to greet the fans. I was surprised because it was a good five or ten minutes after he drove in, plus no one had stopped to greet the fans since Bono did in Oakland almost exactly a month prior. Edge went to the other side of the street to sign autographs, so we didn't think we would get the chance to meet him, but we did! He came to our side of the street and directly toward us. I had met Edge back on Elevation and gotten his autograph, so I just wanted a picture with him. Tasha asked if we could take a photo with him, but he said no. So we shook his hand – his guitar playing hand! I asked him if Larry was coming out. He said, "I can't say for sure. I can't speak for Larry." I thanked him for coming out to greet us, but Tasha said it was too late and I had already offended him. I don't think Edge had a sense of humor about me wanting to meet Larry like Bono did in Seattle and Oakland.

After meeting The Edge, we went into the stadium, went to the bathroom, got a drink and was inside the inner circle by 6pm or so. I started out on Adam's side because that's where Tasha wanted to be, but it was getting too crowded for me where she was standing, so I left when Interpol started. I did not love Interpol, but didn't hate them either. I would see them five more times, as they opened for U2 for the remainder of the U.S. 360 shows. They never did grow on me, but they were alright. I went over to Edge's side of the inner circle because I wanted to watch U2 walk onto the stage, even though there were coming out of the tunnel on Adam's side. I finally got stable video of all four of them walking in and if I'm not mistaken Larry winked and waved to me – that cool, low down by the side of his leg incognito kind of wave.

During the opener "Even Better Than the Real Thing," I made my way back over to Adam's side of the inner circle. Bono said, "Aw yeah ChiTown in the summer. Where ya gonna take us tonight?" Before "The Fly," Bono said, "A whole side of *Achtung Baby* for you." But it wasn't, almost but not quite. During "The Fly," Bono again screamed "Achtung Y'all!" like in the ZooTv days. I can't really explain how excited this makes me! During "Mysterious Ways," Bono sang a snippet from "Trying To Throw Your Arms Around the World." I was really hoping for an all *Achtung Baby* concert at some point in the tour since it was the 20th anniversary, but that never happened.

After "Until the End of the World," instead of "I Will Follow," U2 played "Out of Control" – finally! I had been wanting to hear "Out of Control" the entire tour. It is such a great song, so much energy, so much better than "I Will

Follow." I went nuts as soon as it started! Bono mentioned that it was their first single and he had met the love of his life the same time he met Larry, Edge and Adam. After "Out of Control," U2 went right into "Get On Your Boots." This was an amazing back to back combo of songs full of excitement and energy. It was at this point I knew that the Chicago show was going to be my favorite of the 360 tour – tied with Anaheim2.

After "Get on Your Boots," Bono started talking. This was usually the part where he introduced the band, but he talked about them more than actually introduced them. Bono said that Larry and Adam had been in Chicago for the 4th of July, just as Tasha and I were. Bono said, "Larry watched the White Sox win last night." I knew I should have gone to that White Sox game! Bono introduced "I Still Haven't Found What I'm Looking" For saying, "This is a single off *The Joshua Tree* for Island Records circa 1987." Then in the middle of the song said that John Cusack is in the house, "Happy Birthday John." And at the end, Bono dedicated it to Clarence Clemmons by singing a bit of "Jungle Land," which had been done at the end of "Moment of Surrender" at previous show.
During "Elevation," Bono said, "Take me to the other side. I'm in Larry Mullen's band."

After "Hold Me Thrill Me Kiss Me Kill Me," we went back behind the stage to get a spot to watch U2 walk out – we could see their cars waiting for them in the tunnel. We could also see John Cusack watching the show. After "With or Without You," Bono said that two days ago was the 25th anniversary of Greg Caroll's death and they had written a song about it, but they weren't going to play it. The crowd booed, so Bono said they would discuss it and maybe play it after "Moment of Surrender." They played a snippet of "One Tree Hill" at the end and then Bono said, "Ok here's the deal. If we screw up really badly, you can't put it on the internet. Fair?" Then Edge was trying to figure out how to play it and shouted, "For fuck's sake!" Luckily for us Edge figured it out and U2 played "One Tree Hill" for the first time in the U.S. since 1987. It was amazing, especially when the drums and bass kicked in! I went nuts. *The Joshua Tree* is my favorite album and I didn't see the Joshua Tree tour because I was only 14, so anything played from it is a gift for me!

U2 left the stage and made their way toward us. Adam waved to Tasha. Larry just walked by. As they were almost to their cars, Larry and Adam simultaneously took off their shirts and got into their cars! We walked the two miles from Soldier Field back to our hotel, and so did a lot of other people – there was literally a pedestrian traffic jam. The U2 360 show in Chicago was such a fantastic show! My favorite of the tour, along with Anaheim2. There was a great energy in Soldier Field and the inner circle was really crowded, even where I stood behind the stage.

The set list for the 360 show in Chicago on July 5, 2011 was as follows: Even Better Than The Real Thing, The Fly, Mysterious Ways / Tryin To Throw Your Arms / Independent Women, Until the End of the World, Out Of Control, Get On Your Boots, I Still Haven't Found What I'm Looking For / The Promised Land, Stay – In the Wee Small Hours, Beautiful Day / Space Oddity, Elevation, Pride, Miss Sarajevo, Zooropa, City of Blinding Lights – My Kind of Town, Vertigo, I'll Go Crazy / Discotheque / Life During Wartime, Sunday Bloody Sunday, Scarlet, Walk On – Battle Hymn of the Republic, One, Will You Love Me Tomorrow / Where the Streets Have No Name, Hold Me Thrill Me Kiss Me Kill Me / My Kind of Town, With or Without You, Moment of Surrender / One Tree Hill, One Tree Hill.

Tasha left, and I spent the next day in my hotel room, which is the best way to spend the day after a U2 show. I had a week before my next U2 360 show in Philadelphia.

On the Road to Philadelphia

Day 55 – July 7

While other U2 fans headed to the shows in Montreal, I took a little break. After the fantastic U2 360 show in Chicago on July 5, I rested for a day in the hotel and then headed off to Milwaukee, which was only 90 minutes away. Luckily the fabulous Aloft hotel let us check in at 11:30am. I left the dogs in the room, put my sneakers on and walked around Milwaukee. I walked through the old historic German district to get to my first destination – the Bronz Fonz. My whole reason for visiting Milwaukee was to see the Fonzie statue. *Happy Days* has been my favorite television show since I was little. It took place in Milwaukee, although it wasn't actually filmed there. The Bronz Fonz is on the Riverwalk along the Milwaukee River across from the Rock Bottom Brewery (unfortunately not Shotz Brewery).

After admiring the Bronz Fonz, I talked with a local who told me all about Milwaukee. Then I walked about a mile to Summerfest, which is the largest festival in the world. It goes on for 11 days and has at least five stages. The entire festival was on concrete, so no mud, which I thoroughly appreciated. There were lots of vendors with food (great pizza from Zaffiro's), drinks, clothes, jewelry, etc. It was really great – actually as much of a fair as a music festival. I was there early, so I saw some of the unknown bands but they were very good. I saw Alison Scott from Minneapolis and this great band from Milwaukee. I didn't catch their name, but really enjoyed them. After they performed seven U2 songs were played as they changed the set for the next band: "Pride," "New Year's Day," "With or Without You," "I Still Haven't Found What I'm Looking For," "Sunday Bloody Sunday," "Bad," and "Where the Streets

Have No Name." I of course stayed for all seven songs, even though they were just playing over the speakers. It's like when you can't get out of the car when a U2 song is playing on the radio.

After a few hours walking around Summerfest, I started my mile and a half walk back to the Aloft hotel. I stopped by the Milwaukee Public Market, walked along the Milwaukee River on the Riverwalk and stopped at the Cheese Mart to get dinner. Cheese is my favorite food (pizza my favorite meal), so I really enjoyed the Cheese Mart.

I loved, loved, loved Milwaukee and would move there if it didn't snow from November through March as I am not a fan of winter. It still has the old architecture – not all modern buildings. It isn't crazy crowded with traffic or pedestrians like Chicago. It is a clean city and the people were very nice. I just had a really great feeling there, like it was home. A feeling I've only had on this trip when I was in Palm Springs, similar feeling to what I have when I'm in Memphis and Maryland – home.

Day 56 – July 8

After my beautiful day (and night) in Milwaukee, I left for Canton, Ohio to visit the Pro Football Hall of Fame. I had to drive back through Chicago on my eight-hour drive from Milwaukee to Canton. I arrived at the Hall of Fame just after 3:30. Since it wasn't hot, I parked in the shade and left the dogs in the car while I quickly toured the museum. They were fine as I was only in the Hall of Fame for about an hour because I was really only interested in seeing the Denver Broncos stuff.

The first thing I saw when I walked in the door was a giant photo of my favorite Shannon Sharpe because he was finally being inducted into the Football Hall of Fame that year! They also had Shannon's shoes with "Big Play Shay #84" printed on the tongue and a plaque about Shannon being the #1 Tight End. Reminded me of a sign I made once and took it to the game. It read, "Shannon Sharpe #1 Tight End, #1 in my heart."

My all-time favorite player John Elway was inducted seven years prior to my visit to Canton. There was plenty about Elway in the Hall of Fame including a display about "The Drive," a football commemorating his 50,000 yards passing, a replica of his locker and of course the bronze head for the enshrinement with a plaque about his achievements. I couldn't see Shannon's bronze head because he wasn't inducted until a few weeks after I was at the Hall of Fame. There was also mention of U2's halftime performance at the Super Bowl after 9/11.

Days 57-60 – July 9-12

I spent the next four days after Canton at my parents' house in Ellicott City, Maryland. Unfortunately, my parents weren't there, but it was still a nice little break from the road. On the way home, I stopped at Ledo's for the best pizza in the world! While home I got Big Orange's oil changed, did laundry, got groceries for my final two weeks on the road and had lunch with my best friend and her two daughters.

Day 61 – July 13

I left for Philadelphia exactly two months after I had left Memphis to start my U2 360 Tour Across America, which was also the 26th anniversary of Live Aid also in Philadelphia. I had driven 14,362 miles so far. Growing up in Baltimore, I had been to Philadelphia many, many times, but never to that part of the city. I stayed at the wonderful Hotel Palomar (another Kimpton hotel) in the Arts District surrounded by many shops and restaurants. The staff at the Hotel Palomar was fantastic! They upgraded me to a one bedroom suite for my three night stay, complete with refrigerator, microwave, sleeper sofa, 2 flatscreen tvs, a separate bedroom and living room and a huge bathroom. They framed an 8×10 picture of Elvis and Cilla and left them treats, beds and bowls. They left me bottled water and fruit. It was a great hotel!

After unpacking, organizing and having lunch, I took a cab to Festival Pier at Penn's Landing to see Soundgarden. I bought a fanclub GA ticket, so we were let into the venue before the regular GA. My friend Emily joined me in line. We got to the front rail on the left – Edge side (if Edge were there). Basically the same place I stood last year when I saw Soundgarden at Lollapalooza in Chicago. I was talking with a guy named Andrew who also saw Soundgarden at Lollapalooza last year. He is the lead singer of a band called Shadowplay, which I have come to realize are very good.

After a crazy and an annoying opening band, Mars Volta, Soundgarden took the stage at 8:45. They played my favorites "Spoonman," "My Wave," "Fell on Black Days," "Rusty Cage," and "Black Hole Sun." They were great and seemed really excited the Philly audience was so enthusiastic. Chris Cornell even said something like, 'Finally a real crowd.' Philly concerts are usually really great. About halfway through the show after "Fell on Black Days" (my favorite Soundgarden song), I moved off the front rail. I just couldn't take it anymore. The audience was getting a bit rowdy and there was crowd surfing – not quite the same GA experience as a U2 show. I thought I would move back or to the side to have some room. I kept walking back, but it never cleared out. It was jammed with people everywhere. I think it was more crowded than U2 GA. Festival Pier is just basically a parking lot. There are no seats, just a big concrete area.

The night after the Soundgarden show in Philly was the U2 show in Philly. This would start my last leg of the U2 360 tour, with my final five shows in Philadelphia, St. Louis, New Jersey, Minneapolis and Pittsburgh. I wouldn't be doing any sightseeing though, just driving back and forth to the concerts.

U2 show #71 – July 14, 2011 – Philadelphia

The U2 360 show in Philadelphia was a great show, made even better because I shared it with my old Elevation tour friends as well as couple new friends from the 360 tour. It was especially nice since it was because of the U2 Elevation show in Philadelphia 10 years ago that we became friends. U2 brought back the original version of "Magnificent," not the remix version. They hadn't played "Magnificent" since the first Anaheim show on June 17th. It took the place of "The Fly," but in the sixth spot in the set list rather than the second. U2 ended the show by singing "Happy Birthday" to Nelson Mandela (this was before "Ordinary Love" was written).

On Day 62 of my U2 360 Tour Across America, I took a cab from my fabulous Hotel Palomar in Philly to Lincoln Financial Field around 3pm. I walked around the stadium and ran into my old Elevation friends Ayaz, Kim and Abbey. I finally arrived at the spot where U2 was going to drive in. Along the way, I met up with new friends Christine and Natasha. Christine also lives in Maryland, and Natasha is also a huge Larry fan. My old Elevation friends Jenny and Tasha were also there. U2 drove in after 4pm. Bono came out to greet everyone, but the Philly fans got a little too excited and I couldn't even get near Bono to see him, let alone talk with him. He didn't stay very long, and I don't blame him.

After sort of seeing Bono, Natasha and I walked back around the stadium and went to the front of the GA line to watch everyone enter. I got to talk with my friend Beth for a little bit and catch up a bit with Cathal, author of *Me and U2*. We heard the crew sound check "Breathe" and U2 sound check "Magnificent," so it wasn't a real surprise when they played it. Unfortunately, U2 did not resurrect "Breathe" though. Natasha and I went into the stadium after the GA line filed in. It was quite a complicated walk down to the inner circle, which was already pretty crowded at 5:30. In fact, Adam's side was closed.

We went into Edge's side of the inner circle and stood behind the stage to get our spot to watch U2 enter the stadium and go on stage. Rob, another friend from the Elevation days, joined us. Jenny and I were wearing our "Larry Mullen Band" shirts and Natasha was wearing her "It's All About Drums" shirt. Dallas said Hello, shook my hand and complimented me on my hat and then said, "It's not about the drums, it's about the guitar." When opening band Interpol walked on stage which wasn't until after 7:45, the drummer noticed our shirts and pointed at us. Then after their set when they were walking off stage, the drummer gave his drumsticks to Jenny and said, "This is for my love of Larry."

There were again issues with venue security moving us away from where U2 walked onto the stage, but we found Rocco and he straightened it out again for us like he did in Anaheim. It's great that U2 and their crew really care about their fans. I just wish they would communicate better with venue security. There always seem to be two sets of rules. The inner circle was especially crowded. People were even in my spot on the back rail behind the stage. It was great to watch the show with my new friend Natasha and my old Elevation friends Jenny, Paola, Gina and Rob.

The Philly 360 show was the standard set list, except for the replacement of "The Fly" with the original "Magnificent," "Hallelujah" into "Streets" *(*first time I had heard that*)* and "Happy Birthday" to Nelson Mandela – even though it was four days away and may have made more sense to sing it at the St. Louis show. At the end of "Mysterious Ways," Bono sang, "Young American. Philadelphia." During "Until the End of the World," Bono said, "Bass and Drums!" and then "Love and Peace!" I love it when he says "Love and Peace!" It reminds me of the Vertigo tour with Larry banging his drum and screaming "RELEASE! RELEASE! RELEASE!" I have a Love and Peace drum pin from the Hard Rock and my Christmas card that year read "Peace, Love, Joy."

After "Magnificent," Bono said, "Wow! That is a great start! Thank you SO much! Philadelphia!" There weren't really any extensive band introductions. Bono just named everyone and again thanked the fans for their patience while he was recovering from his back surgery the previous year. He commented on what a special unity there is between U2 and their fans. He did say they were in the home of the Philadelphia Eagles, to which I booed loudly. I don't think Bono knows that the team is led by a dog killer. During "City of Blinding Lights," Bono sang, "City of brotherly and sisterly blinding lights." During "Walk On," Bono said, "A message of love from the city of brotherly love all the way to Asia."

At the end of the show, we went back toward tunnel where U2 would exit. Larry again took off his shirt on the way to his car. On the way out of the stadium, I caught up with my new friend Steve. It didn't take too long to get a cab back to the hotel. U2 ended at 11:30, and I was back at my hotel by 12:30.

The set list for the 360 show in Philadelphia on July 14, 2011 was as follows: Even Better Than The Real Thing, I Will Follow, Mysterious Ways, Until the End of the World, Get On Your Boots, Magnificent, I Still Haven't Found What I'm Looking For, Stay, Beautiful Day / Space Oddity, Elevation, Pride, Miss Sarajevo, Zooropa, City of Blinding Lights, Vertigo / It's Only Rock and Roll, I'll Go Crazy / Discotheque / Life

During Wartime / Psycho Killer, Sunday Bloody Sunday, Scarlet, Walk On, One, Hallelujah / Where the Streets Have No Name, Hold Me Thrill Me Kiss Me Kill Me, With or Without You, Moment of Surrender, Happy Birthday.

The day after the U2 show I relaxed in my lovely suite at the Hotel Palomar in Philadelphia before my long 16-hour drive to St. Louis for the next U2 360 show.

On the Road to St. Louis

Day 64 – July 16

The morning after the U2 show, we left Philadelphia just after 6am est driving the Pennsylvania Turnpike – again. I was on that dreaded $20-toll turnpike the week before and two weeks before that, and would be driving it again in a few days and again the following week. Ugh! But I did come across a historical marker at the one of the first travel stops on the PA Turnpike, so at least that was something interesting.

We stopped four times for gas, food, etc in addition to the two times we were stopped in traffic. Both traffic jams were on Route 70 West in Indiana about two hours apart, which was very frustrating. It was truly Carmageddon everywhere that day in July – the 405 in Southern California was closed, Route 240 in Memphis was down to one lane, and Route 70 West in Indiana was shut down twice. If I hadn't been delayed, I would not have seen the beautiful sunset. There is always good that comes with the bad.

We finally arrived at our great Drury Plaza Hotel in St. Louis just past 9:30pm cst, over 16 hours and almost 900 miles later. My drive from Anaheim to Baltimore was easier than that drive from Philadelphia to St. Louis. Elvis and Cilla were exhausted! As soon as I walked into the lobby, I realized this was the hotel I stayed at when I visited St. Louis eight years prior when I went to the Orioles-Cardinals game. The staff was fantastic! They answered my questions immediately and quickly brought me what I needed, as well as checked me in quickly knowing I had a long day. To reward myself for my rough day of driving, I ordered a pizza from Imo's for a late dinner. It was "an original St. Louis style pizza." I didn't even know there was a 'St. Louis style' pizza. It is a very thin crust with provolone cheese, but it tasted like cheddar was mixed in with it. It was no Ledo's, but it was really, really good.

U2 show #72 – July 17, 2011 – St. Louis

The U2 360 show in St. Louis was amazing! It was definitely one of my favorites of the tour, along with Chicago and Anaheim2. Even though it was a standard set list, there was no "Out of Control" or "One Tree Hill," the band and the audience had such a great energy. Bono was especially excited and happy. "The Fly" returned after its brief departure in Philadelphia, and "Magnificent" disappeared again. For the first time, both Bono and Larry acknowledged me on their way onto the stage and then later Bono gave me an indirect 'shout out' during the band introductions. The St. Louis show was the hottest show of the U.S. tour, beating Baltimore, Nashville and New Jersey with its 110 heat index.

On Day 65 of my U2 360 Tour Across America, my friend Beth flew in on the morning of the show. We talked the day before as she made last minute plans to come to St. Louis, so we decided that she would share the hotel room with Elvis, Cilla and myself. We relaxed in the hotel for a bit, then went to lunch on the way to Busch Stadium, which was only a couple blocks away from our hotel. We had a great pasta lunch at Caleco's thinking we should carb up to sustain the long day in the hot sun and 110 degree heat!

After lunch, we made our way to Busch Stadium to try to figure out where U2 would drive in. Luckily, the spot we chose was in the shade. My friend Chuck and Beth's friend Tim were there. We also ran into Cathal and a few others. There was a bit of discrepancy where the band was actually going to drive in. There were a lot of people on the other side of the stadium waiting, and only about 10 of us on our side. Turned out we were right and the band drove in just after 5p where we were waiting. Bono rolled down his window and waved, and Edge and Adam waved from inside their cars. About 15 minutes or so later, another car drove in. It was Larry and he waved. We were surprised when no one came out to greet us, since there were only about 10 of us there.

I walked into the stadium and over to the inner circle on Edge's side, but it was closed. So I had to walk around to Adam's side, get my stamp for re-entry, then walk back over to Edge's side. Even though I could see that U2 was going to walk into the stadium from the tunnel on Adam's side, I wanted to be on Edge's side so I could watch them walk onto the stage, or under the stage actually. My friend Jason from Memphis joined me. He had contacted me earlier and drove up that afternoon and luckily bought a GA from someone outside the stadium around 6pm. I met a guy and his young son Tyler, I mean like seven years old young, who had been to nine shows this tour. Turned out, they read my blog and Tyler's favorites are Larry and Bono – as our mine. A guy from the crew asked me how many shows I had been to. When I told him all the U.S. shows that leg and I was driving to all of them with my dogs, he said I was crazy and should just give my money to him. I told him I should work for U2, so I could get paid to follow the tour. Apparently, my resume got lost in the mail because Larry has yet to call me for a job.

Interpol took the stage around 7:30m and played their usual set. I still was not a fan, but they were ok. U2 didn't come out until about 9:15pm. On the way to the stage, Larry saw me and smiled and waved. And not his usual obligatory smile and wave, but he actually seemed to recognize and acknowledge me. Then Bono smiled, waved and said 'Hi' to me. I could definitely see recognition in his face – and it's been a long time since I spoke with him in Seattle and Oakland. So maybe Bono and Larry were actually waving to me as they drove into the stadium earlier. Or it could have been the fact that I was almost always standing at that same spot where U2 walk onto the stage and always wearing my straw cowboy hat and 'Larry Mullen Band' shirt. Yeah maybe after 12 shows, they finally recognize me.

My excitement grew even greater when U2 followed the opener "Even Better Than the Real Thing" with "The Fly," which they had removed from the set list in Philadelphia and replaced it with "Magnificent." Introducing "The Fly" Bono said, "Are you ready for some crowd rock circa 1991? We're not gonna walk, we're not gonna crawl. Tonight St. Louis, we Fly!" It was at that moment, I knew the St. Louis show was going to be one of my favorite 360 shows. U2 had such a great energy, and Bono seemed especially excited and happy. As always, "The Fly" was followed by "Mysterious Ways" and "Until the End of the World." I just love four straight opening songs off *Achtung Baby*. I am sorry for the people who missed the first U.S. leg of the 360 Tour in 2009 and didn't get to hear the great new songs off *No Line on the Horizon,* but I loved hearing all the old *Achtung Baby* songs on its 20th anniversary. Like going back to Zoo Tv.

The inner circle wasn't that crowded, so I moved from my usual spot behind the stage and stood toward the side of the stage during "Until the End of the World" and "I Will Follow" and actually got pictures of the whole band.

During "Until the End of the World," Bono again said "Bass and Drums" and then "Love and Peace." He went on to say, "What sort of magic night is this? St. Louis, Missouri. Warm summer night." During "I Will Follow," Bono said the most important word of the night was 'surrender.' He sang, "I surrender. St. Louis. We surrender."

As if I wasn't excited enough, or hot enough, from "Get on Your Boots," one of my favorite parts of the 360 show, Bono started his usual talk before "I Still Haven't Found What I'm Looking For." He read the set list from a show U2 played in St. Louis 30 years prior. I thought they would play an impromptu old song, especially when everyone cheered when he read "Out of Control," but they didn't. Bono started the band introductions. He said, "So much has changed and yet so much remains the same. Larry is still upset about the fact that we changed our name to U2 from the Larry Mullen Band. And there are some people here who agree with him." With that Larry busted out laughing. After the show, everyone told me Bono was referring to me, and maybe he was since both he and Larry did clearly notice me on the way to the stage. So I am going to believe that was my shout out from Bono.

That St. Louis show was so hot and humid that Bono took off his signature jacket during the second or third song and performed in his tee shirt. Then he left Edge to introduce "Stay" while he went down into the underworld to change his shirt. During "Beautiful Day" Bono shouted," Turn the lights on Willie. I want to see these people." Then during "Elevation," Bono brought up some new U2 fans on stage. As hot as it was, U2 chose the St. Louis show to wear their lighted jackets during "Zooropa" and "City of Blinding Lights." I love Larry in that black jacket (it's so Elvis), but I can't believe they chose the hottest show of the tour to wear them. In the past, it had only been at the colder shows out West. During "City of Blinding Lights," Bono brought up a young boy with him to run around the cat walk – again during the hottest show of the tour.

It was so hot that Adam went shirtless under his jacket during "I'll Go Crazy If I Don't Go Crazy Tonight." After watching Larry start "I'll Go Crazy," turn around facing the back during "Sunday Bloody Sunday," and his drum solo during "Scarlet," I walked around to Adam's side of the inner circle to watch the rest of the show. Even though I like Edge's side better, I knew U2 would leave through the tunnel on Adam's side of the inner circle. As they walked by very quickly, I shouted out to Larry and he waved and smiled, but at my friend Chuck not at me.

July 17th was the 8th anniversary of my beloved Grandmother's death, so maybe Grandmom had a hand in making that U2 360 show in St. Louis special for me. It was a great night! A fantastic show! One of my favorites! People who weren't there have asked me why the St. Louis show was better than the others because there wasn't anything extraordinary about the set list. It is hard to really put into words unless you were there. It was just a feeling we all had who were at the show. There was an amazing energy that hot night in St. Louis!

The set list from the 360 show in St. Louis on July 17, 2011 was as follows: Even Better Than The Real Thing, The Fly, Mysterious Ways, Until the End of the World, I Will Follow, Get On Your Boots, I Still Haven't Found What I'm Looking For / Many Rivers to Cross, Stay, Beautiful Day / Space Oddity, Elevation, Pride, Miss Sarajevo, Zooropa, City of Blinding Lights, Vertigo, I'll Go Crazy / Discotheque / Life During Wartime – Psycho Killer, Sunday Bloody Sunday, Scarlet, Walk On, One, Hallelujah / Where the Streets Have No Name, Hold Me Thrill Me Kiss Me Kill Me, With or Without You, Moment of Surrender.

On the Road to New Jersey

Days 66-67 – July 18-19

After the horrible days I had driving from Miami to Nashville in one day and Philadelphia to St. Louis in one day, I had learned my lesson and decided to break up the drive from St. Louis to New Jersey into two days. I left St. Louis around noon the day after the fantastic U2 show. In fact, it was so fantastic that I didn't get much sleep, so I only drove about 350 miles to Dayton, Ohio. I originally wanted to make it to Columbus, which was only about another hour, but I just couldn't do it. I ordered an amazing pizza from Donatos (thin crust with lots and lots of cheese), settled into my Motel 6 hotel room, and watched Bono and Edge on Letterman. Unfortunately, I didn't get much sleep that night either and I had to drive 600 miles to New Jersey. I left Dayton at 6am, stopped twice, drove across the Pennsylvania turnpike again and arrived in our Homestead Suites hotel across the street from the New Meadowlands stadium.

U2 show #73 – July 20, 2011 – East Rutherford

The U2 360 show in East Rutherford, New Jersey was the longest of the U.S. tour at two and a half hours. The show included two extra songs. U2 played "Out of Control," not instead of "I Will Follow" like usual but in addition to. They also played both "The Fly," in its typical second spot, and "Magnificent," after "Get on Your Boots" which was a first. And as in Philadelphia, it was the original album version of "Magnificent," not the remix of the earlier shows. And Edge came out to greet the fans before the show.

I finally got a great night's sleep the night before the U2 show in Jersey and also took a nap a couple hours after I woke up. I was very tired. On Day 68 of my U2 360 Tour Across America, I was awakened by the fire alarm going off, which was luckily a false alarm. After the impromptu fire drill, I followed my normal show day routine of watching tv, ordering lunch, walking the dogs before going to the stadium.

Even though I was at the Homestead Suites across the street from the New Meadowlands Stadium, I couldn't walk there because of the highway, so luckily the Sheraton next door had a shuttle going over. I thought that would be easier than driving over myself and parking, but I was wrong. It was $20 for one person, since I didn't want to wait until after 5pm to go over. I had to be there when U2 arrived because I knew the one time I wasn't there, Larry would stop just as he had in Jersey ten years prior on the Elevation Tour. I wasn't going to miss him twice!

I picked up my red zone ticket and wristband and walked around to where everyone was waiting for U2 to arrive. Quite a large crowd had already gathered to wait for U2. I hung out with my new friends Anisha and Dafna. U2 finally arrived, well everyone except Larry. Paul McGuinness drove in, then Adam, then Edge and then Bono. Edge came out to greet everyone as he did in Chicago. I walked around and asked Jerry in security if Larry would stop to sign, but he just smiled and said he didn't know. I waited forever for Larry to arrive. Not sure why he didn't arrive with the rest of the band. About two hours later around 6:30 or so, Larry finally arrived. There were still a few of us left waiting, but he didn't stop.

For the only time on that leg of the tour, I had a Red Zone ticket. It was on Adam's side of the stage. I left to watch U2 walk in as I always do, but I didn't want to walk all the way around to Edge's side to watch them walk onto the stage because the sun had really worn me out. So I just stayed on

Adam's side because they were walking out of the tunnel on his side. I ran into Mike, my oldest U2 friend – from *The Joshua Tree* days in high school. We saw a set list someone had that said the encore was "Out of Control," "Bad," and "40" closing the show, but we didn't believe it. Interpol didn't come on until about 7:45. I realized the lead singer must be an Elvis fan. He had Elvis-like sunglasses and said, 'Thank you very much.' I liked their first two songs, but then his voice started to get on my nerves.

    It was pretty exciting to watch U2 walk all the way down the tunnel – usually I just see them walking up to the stage. I could have sworn that when Larry and Adam emerged from the tunnel, they saw me (because I was directly in front of them and don't really blend in with the crowd) and Larry sort of jokingly hid behind Adam grabbing him as if to say, 'oh no there she is again!' No I really don't actually think I am that present in Larry's mind, but it is fun to believe it every now and again.

    After U2 walked by, I ran over to the Red Zone to watch the show. It seemed I was a bit more excited than everyone else there, especially when U2 added an extra song, "Magnificent," after "Get on Your Boots." The Red Zone was more crowded than I thought it would be. I stood two people back from the catwalk and had a side view of the stage, so I could see everything. I still liked my spot behind the stage better though. It's closer and had a better view of Larry. Also, Bono and Edge go behind the stage more than they come over to the catwalk on Adam's side where I was. The Red Zone was great for "I'll Go Crazy if I Don't Go Crazy Tonight" though. I got to see Adam, Edge and Larry up close.

    During "Even Better Than the Real Thing," Bono said, "Jersey on a hot summer night. Where you going to take us?" Even though St. Louis was way hotter than Jersey, Bono only called St. Louis a 'warm summer night.' Bono commented all night how hot it was in New Jersey (not even 90 degrees), even though it was much hotter in St. Louis (110 degrees) a few days earlier. I think he was still overheated from St. Louis. Bono again introduced "The Fly" as "crowd rock circa 1991." Bono was really into "The Fly" – almost angrily screaming the lyrics. At the end of "Mysterious Ways," Bono again threw in a little "Trying to Throw Your Arms Around the World" as he had done in Chicago, but very little this time with "going to run to you run to you run to you." During "Until the End of the World" Bono said, "Love and Peace" but no 'bass and drums.' Bono again said the most special word of the night was 'surrender' during "I Will Follow" saying, "I surrender. We surrender." After "Magnificent," which was played after "Get on Your Boots" for the first time, Bono said, "Magnificent new stadium. We have played East Rutherford 24 times." I realize I have been to nine of those East Rutherford shows.

As he had done at the St. Louis show, Bono read a set list from 30 years ago. Also just like in St. Louis, Bono said, "Some things change but so much remains the same in this band. I'd like to point out that Larry Mullen is still trying to figure out why it's called U2 and not the Larry Mullen Band. And I think he has a point. We're very grateful Sir for taking us off the streets of Dublin. Thank you." But this time no mention indirectly of me. During "I Still Haven't Found What I'm Looking For" Bono said, "We want to thank Father Springsteen for the lend of the hall and some other things besides. Thank you Bruce." Just like at the St. Louis show, Edge spoke before "Stay" while Bono changed his shirt and then started to play "Stuck in a Moment" by accident. Too bad, I would rather
hear "Stuck" than "Stay." During "Elevation" Bono said, "So hot tonight I feel like I could die." After "Pride," the audience kept singing the "oh oh oh ohs" for quite some time and Bono said, "Noisy New Jersey." Before "Miss Sarajevo" Bono said, "If

you're Irish, this is really hot." Again, it was much hotter at the St. Louis show.

After "I'll Go Crazy," I left the Red Zone for my usual spot behind the stage and felt right at home. It was less crowded and I was closer to Larry – and closer to Bono when he came back for "Sunday Bloody Sunday" and "Streets." Someone rushed the stage from behind on Edge's side during "Streets." I saw Sammy and security run after him, but couldn't see what happened. It figures one of the few shows I'm not on Edge's side that happened. After "Walk On" Bono said, "Oh my God New Jersey thank you!"

During "With or Without You," I walked back toward the tunnel to wait for U2 to leave. Paul McGuinness was standing behind me watching the show. Bono said, "Feeling a little faint earlier. I hope you don't mind. It's hot here!" Bono dedicated "Moment of Surrender" to the E Street Band and Bruce. After "Moment of Surrender," U2 walked to the front of the stage and took their bows. I was of course watching Larry and saw him lean to Bono and say something like, 'Do you want to play another one? It's up to you.' Then Bono said, "Let's do one more." I heard the beginning of "Out of Control" and ran back to the stage, since some folks had left I was able to stand up front at the side of the stage. It was SO great!

After "Out of Control," I went back to the stairs to watch U2 walk off stage and then I ran back toward the tunnel to watch them leave. As Edge and Bono approached the tunnel, they hugged this man. Security said it was Bruce Springsteen, but I didn't think it looked like him. I had to wait over an hour to catch the shuttle back to my hotel after the show. The entire parking lot was almost empty before we got on the shuttle back to the hotel. It figured that the longest show of the U.S. tour coupled with an unfortunate late shuttle happened the night before I had to get up and drive halfway to Minneapolis for the next U2 show.

The set list for the 360 show in New Jersey on July 20, 2011 was as follows: Even Better Than The Real Thing, The Fly, Mysterious Ways, Until the End of the World / Anthem, I Will Follow, Get On Your Boots, Magnificent, I Still Haven't Found What I'm Looking For / Promised Land, Stay / In the Wee Small Hours, Beautiful Day / Space Oddity, Elevation, Pride, Miss Sarajevo, Zooropa, City of Blinding Lights, Vertigo, I'll Go Crazy / Discotheque / Psycho Killer / Life During Wartime, Sunday Bloody Sunday, Scarlet, Walk On, One, Hallelujah / Where the Streets Have No Name, Hold Me Thrill Me Kiss Me Kill Me, With or Without You, Moment of Surrender / Jungleland, Out of Control.

After the New Jersey show, I didn't feel like it was that great of a show. I remember being really excited for "Out of Control" of course, but just thought it was the typical U2 show – nothing particularly extraordinary. But after listening to the bootleg, that U2 360 show in New Jersey was really good. U2 really did end with four fantastic shows in the US – St. Louis, New Jersey, Minneapolis, Pittsburgh.

On the Road to Minneapolis

Days 69 – July 21

With just under a week remaining in my U2 360 Tour Across America, I was exhausted as I drove from New Jersey to Minnesota. Again driving back through Pennsylvania and Ohio where I had just driven a few days before. I left the morning after the U2 show in New Jersey, just before 11am, and drove 443 miles to a Motel 6 in Richfield, Ohio arriving around 6:30pm. I had to stop twice along the way to stay awake and didn't drive as far as I originally wanted.

Day 70 – July 22

The next morning I left bright and early at 7am to make my way to Minneapolis for the second to last U2 show on my 360 tour. I spent over $18. on the Ohio and Indiana Turnpikes and was stuck in traffic for over an hour getting around Chicago. There was so much construction all the way through Illinois. After stopping once in Illinois and once in Wisconsin, I finally arrived at the Days Hotel in Minneapolis 13 ½ hours and 754 miles later. I ordered a pizza and went to bed.

U2 show #74 – July 23, 2011 – Minneapolis

On Day 71 of my U2 360 Tour Across America, I stayed in bed all day before walking over to TCF Bank Stadium at the University of Minnesota at 2pm. Luckily my hotel was right next to the stadium, just as it had been in Denver. It was a bright sunny day when I left, but they were calling for rain. With the exception of a short sprinkle at the end of the Chicago show, it had not rained at any of the 14 shows I had been to so far on my 360 tour. I walked around the entire stadium trying to figure out where U2 would drive in. I thought it might be this spot in the back, but continued around to the other side of the GA line where I saw the crew going in and out and a bunch of fans waiting. I hung out with my new friends Stuart, Jason, Tim, Cathal and Suzi. Apparently, I should have followed my instinct and stayed in that spot around the back of the stadium where I thought U2 would drive in because that's where they came in and I missed them, but no one stopped anyway. That was only the second time I had missed U2 arrive at the stadium. The other time was in East Lansing.

I went into the show around 6pm and went to Edge's side of the inner circle, so I could watch U2 walk to the stage, even though they were entering from the tunnel on Adam's side. I prefered to watch U2 walk in and go under the stage, which was on Edge's side. Deb and her husband were already there waiting. We ended up hanging out throughout the entire show, which was great fun. While were waiting for Interpol to take the stage, a guy from the crew told us they have names for each of us, but he wouldn't tell us what they were as I am sure they were not flattering. He said they even play bingo and mark off spaces when they see us at a show. I told him to tell Larry I've been to every U.S. show that leg and was anxious to meet him. He said he hadn't even met Larry.

While waiting for U2 to take the stage, I met Jill and her friends who were also at the shows in Anaheim. My new friend Shelly was sitting behind the stage, shouted down to me and took a picture of me waiting behind the stage. It was unfortunate that we didn't get a chance to actually talk in Minneapolis, but we have become friends since. She was kind enough to make me audio copies of all 16 U2 shows I traveled to. As U2 walked toward the stage and made that turn to go into the underworld, Larry saw me and smiled and waved just like he did in St. Louis. I sort of captured it on video, but didn't get a picture of it. Shelly told me after that she saw Larry wave to me, so I know I'm not imagining it.

During "Even Better Than the Real Thing" Bono said, "Come on now. The Twin Cities. Where are you going to take us tonight? Minneapolis. St. Paul." To introduce "The Fly" Bono said, "Ya'll want to hear some crowd rock circa 1991? *Achtung Baby* etc." It started to rain toward the end of "Mysterious Ways." Bono said, "Rain come. Love like rain. Love like rain comes in the summer." Bono introduced "Until the End of the World" saying, "Are you ready for this rain dance?" The rain caused Edge to have guitar issues, and he couldn't make it out onto the bridge when Bono was waiting for him. Because of the umbrellas above the drum kit, Larry and Bono could not stand back to back during my favorite "LET ME IN THE SOUND!" during "Get on Your Boots." Bono finished the song by saying, "Get on your boots in your fancy new stadium."

    Before the band introductions, Bono mentioned that Minneapolis was originally supposed to be the last show of the tour, then they added two more shows. He said, "This is the place to begin the end of the tour party." Bono talked about how the past few shows had been some of the best. He said, "The last show I thought I heard thunder, and I felt like a flash of lightening. Then I felt like a truck had hit me. Then I thought I've got into the ring with Mike Tyson. He's beating me in the back of my head. But it was none of those things. It was Larry Mullen Jr on the drums!" There was a huge applause, more than usual for Larry. Minneapolis really likes Larry! After "I Still Haven't Found What I'm Looking For," U2 launched into a full version of "Stand By Me." During which, Bono brought Somali pop star K'naan on stage to sing with them. Apparently, Bono had spoken with K'naan before the show about the famine in Somalia.

    U2 played "Stuck in a Moment" instead of "Stay" – yay! Bono introduced "Stuck" saying, "We wrote this next song for Michael Hutchence, but you will understand if tonight we play it for Amy Winehouse." Amy Winehouse had died earlier that day. At the end of "Pride," the audience kept singing the 'Oh Oh Ohs' and Bono said, "That's a beautiful sound. The sound of America in the rain singing its heart out." It had been raining since "Mysterious Ways," but when "Zooropa" started it was really pouring – a cold sideways rain of huge drops. I remember full out dancing with Deb and her husband in the pouring rain. It was so freeing and fun. Some people had left or were standing under the bridges, but if U2 were playing their hearts out in the rain on the stage, I was going to give them back that same energy.

Unfortunately, the rain did cause some problems for Larry. He seemed to be uncomfortable as he was constantly adjusting his seat throughout the show. And because of the umbrellas, Larry's drum kit didn't turn around during "Sunday Bloody Sunday" – much to my disappointment. Bono wore his army green hat during the encores. I did not walk around to Adam's side after "Scarlet" as I usually did to wait for U2 to leave because I was afraid I would fall in the pouring rain on the way over. The flooring in the stadium was very slick in the rain. Instead, I stood at the stairs and watched U2 leave the stage. Larry again saw me and smiled and waved.

The U2 show in Minneapolis was great – a fantastic energy much like it was in St. Louis. The rain didn't damper the experience at all. In fact, it made it even better – and my hat survived the downpour. The rain began during the third song "Mysterious Ways" and continued throughout the show, raining harder and harder and lightning during the encore. It ended my 'no rain' streak – 14 shows on the last leg of the 360 tour with no rain. The highlights for me were a full performance of "Stand By Me" with K'naan, "Stuck in a Moment" instead of "Stay," and of course Larry smiling and waving to me as he walked on stage and as he left the stage. It was a great show, even though "Magnificent" was not played.

The set list for the 360 show in Minneapolis on July 23, 2011 was as follows: Even Better Than the Real Thing, The Fly, Mysterious Ways / Rain, Until the End of the World / Anthem, I Will Follow, Get On Your Boots, I Still Haven't Found, Stand By Me, Stuck in a Moment, Beautiful Day / Space Oddity, Can't Stand the Rain – Elevation, Pride, Miss

Sarajevo, Zooropa, City of Blinding Lights / Singing in the Rain, Vertigo, Miss You / I'll Go Crazy / Raindrops Keep Falling / Discotheque / Life During Wartime / Psycho Killer, Please / Sunday Bloody Sunday, Scarlet, Walk On, One / Purple Rain, Hallelujah / Purple Rain / Where the Streets Have No Name / Singing in the Rain, Hold Me Thrill Me Kiss Me Kill Me, With or Without You, Moment of Surrender / Singing in the Rain.

The next morning I would leave for my last show and my last chance to meet Larry. I had already seen 15 great U2 shows and had shaken Larry's hand in Seattle as he was leaving the stage, so whatever happened at the show in Pittsburgh would be icing on the cake. Little did I know, it would be the most amazing, delicious icing I had ever had!

On the Road to Pittsburgh

Days 72-73 – July 24-25

I left Minneapolis just before 11am the morning after the U2 show. I was in a great mood because it was such a great show, but I was exhausted. I stopped one time in Wisconsin before stopping for the night at a Motel 6 in Joliet, Illinois. The next day I drove through Indiana and Ohio, again, and made it to Pittsburgh for my final show of the U2 360 tour. I had driven 16,888 miles since I left Memphis 73 days prior. Neil McCormick was showing *Killing Bono* that night in the Pittsburgh area, but I was too exhausted to go. Plus I had already seen it at the Seattle Film Festival in June.

U2 show #75 – July 26, 2011 – Pittsburgh

Day 74 of my U2 360 Tour Across America was also my last. That U2 show in Pittsburgh was my final 360 show, my 16th of that leg, my 24th of the tour, and my 75th U2 show overall. It couldn't have ended better if I would have scripted it myself. It was more than I could have hoped for, more than I ever imagined – Larry hugged me on his way to the stage! So the first few songs on my last U2 360 show were pretty much a blur. It was a standard set list but then U2 ended the show with "Bad," one of my favorite U2 songs. U2 had not played it in the U.S. since that first show in Chicago in 2009. I was happy "Bad" was the last song I heard U2 perform. After the show when Larry walked off the stage and toward the tunnel, he saw me, smiled and gave me a thumbs up – twice. I was so happy Larry smiling at me was the last image I have of the U2 360 tour.

I began the day in Pittsburgh just as I had for the previous 15 U2 360 shows. I walked the dogs, ate breakfast, watched tv, napped, ordered lunch and went to the stadium in the afternoon to wait for U2 to arrive. I met my friends Abbey and Anisha in the lobby of my hotel the Wyndham Grand Pittsburgh, and we took the free shuttle over to the stadium at 2pm, even though it was close enough to walk. It was a beautiful day, in the 80s, sunny, breezy, and not humid. I saw many friends old and new, including Jennifer and Chris, Tyler and his dad, Tim, and Sarah. But the surprise was Matt, Melissa, her parents and Kim. I had no idea they were coming and very happy to see them, and it turned out to be very fortunate for me as well.

U2 arrived just around 5pm. Bono and Edge came out to greet the fans. I couldn't get close enough to talk with them, but I did see Larry and Adam get out of their cars and walk inside. Matt and Melissa talked with Bono and selflessly told him about me and how I had driven to every U.S. show and would like to meet Larry. Brian, Bono's security guy, told them to wait there and he would see what he could do.

Brian came out later and told me Larry was in a meeting, but he told Larry about me and then Bono told Larry about me. I was freaking out imagining Larry being told about me, that I was even in his thoughts for a second! Not sure if they realized I was me. Maybe Bono and Larry knew Brian was talking about me, since I talked with Bono in Seattle and Oakland about meeting Larry, and Larry sometimes waved to me as he walked to the stage. Brian said he recognized me at the shows. Brian took my phone number and said he would look for us inside. My phone number? Was Larry going to call me? Larry now has my phone number? What would I say? I can just imagine the caller id!

Brian gave all of us wristbands for the VIP soundboard area as well as for the Red Zone, but I didn't use them. I went to my usual spot on Edge's side of the inner circle to wait for U2 to enter. Abbey was with me. Deb and her husband and Melissa's parents were also there. Melissa and Matt stood on Adam's side of the stage. Brian came over and told me that he was still working on getting me to meet Larry. Interpol didn't take the stage until about 7:45 and played their usual set.

I'm not sure when U2 came out, probably just about 9pm. When they walked out of the tunnel (on Adam's side) I noticed Larry wasn't first as usual. Adam and Edge were first and Larry and Bono were behind them, so I kind of thought something was up. Then somehow Larry moved up front. As Larry walked up the ramp, he locked eyes with me and was smiling, then he looked down. Larry walked across the platform, jumped down to me, and hugged me. He didn't say a word. Larry just put his arms around me. It felt like the hug lasted forever, but in reality it was only a few seconds. Larry definitely pulled away first because I kept hanging on. I think I muttered a 'thank you' as he preed himself off of me.

Larry gave me the biggest, best hug ever and then went on stage. I burst into tears, as I am doing now while writing this. My friends around me congratulated me and hugged me, which made the moment even more special. I was so excited that I don't really remember "Even Better Than the Real Thing" or "The Fly" – thank goodness for bootlegs. I don't think I became conscious again until "Mysterious Ways" when Larry's drum kit turned around and faced me behind the stage. I never in a million years thought Larry would walk over to me and hug me on his way to the stage before the show. He does not do stuff like that. Maybe once every ten years. First walking to the front of the stage during the show in Providence in 2001 to give me his champagne bottle, and now in 2011 hugging me on his way to the stage on the last 360 show in the U.S.

During "Even Better Than the Real Thing" Bono said, "Hot summer night in the Burgh!" Bono introduced "The Fly" saying, "Some crowd rock circa 1991! Achtung Ya'll!" Instead of singing "Until the End of the World," I kept singing "You were acting like it was the end of the tour" to Abbey. During the band introductions, Bono said, "This is the last night of the 360 Tour in the United States. We've had some cool people come out of our town. Would you say behind me you might call this man the Charles Bronson of U2? Larry Mullen on the drums. Our very own movie star."

U2 again wore their LED jackets during "Zooropa" and "City of Blinding Lights." I love Larry in that black, leather, 1950s Elvis looking jacket. He should always wear black! At the end of "Vertigo," Bono sang a snippet of "Two Hearts Beat as One." During "I'll Go Crazy if I Don't Go Crazy Tonight," Larry looked at me and I shouted "Thank you!" What a dork I am. At the end of "Where the

Streets Have No Name" Bono shouted, "Tuesday night in the old steel town!" I decided to go over to Adam's side of the inner circle during "Hold Me Thrill Me Kiss Me Kill Me" so I could watch U2 leave.

As "With or Without You" started, Bono brought my friends Matt and Melissa on stage and said, "60 shows. Matt and Melissa. Where love stories begin." Matt and Melissa met during Elevation, got engaged during Vertigo and got married during 360. Matt and Melissa slow danced while U2 played. It was beautiful! After "Moment of Surrender," U2 took their bows, huddled together and then played "Bad" with a little snippet of "40" at the end! It was fantastic, a perfect way to end my last show! The song lasted for almost nine minutes. Bono dedicated "Bad" to Andy Rowen who was at the show and whom the song was written about. Andy Rowen is the brother of Bono's friend Guggi and the brother of Peter, who is on the cover of "Boy."

As U2 were walking off stage, I could have sworn I saw Larry looking for me on Edge's side where I was when he hugged me at the beginning of the show. But when they were almost at the tunnel, Larry saw me, smiled and gave me a thumbs up – twice. It looked as if Larry was going to walk over to me, but then he was ushered toward the tunnel by security. After the show I saw Chuck and Tasha and told them about Larry hugging me and then I met up with Beth and shared my story with her. I walked back to the hotel alone (with thousands of other happy U2 fans) across the bridge looking back at the 360 claw for the last time. I got back to the hotel and talked with Patty and her husband. Then I took Elvis and Cilla outside where Abbey met us. We chatted for a bit then I went back inside and wrote in my journal about my last night on the U2 360 tour. I barely slept that night, only three hours.

The set list of my final U2 360 show in Pittsburgh on July 26, 2011 was as follows: Even Better Than the Real

Thing, The Fly, Mysterious Ways / Someone Somewhere in Summertime / Promised You a Miracle, Until the End of the World / Anthem, I Will Follow, Get On Your Boots, I Still Haven't Found / The Promised Land, Stay, Beautiful Day / Space Oddity, Elevation, Pride, Miss Sarajevo, Zooropa, City of Blinding Lights, Vertigo / Two Hearts Beat As One, Miss You / I'll Go Crazy / Discotheque / Psycho Killer / Life During Wartime / Please, Sunday Bloody Sunday, Scarlet, Walk On, One, Hallelujah / Where The Streets Have No Name, Hold Me Thrill Me Kiss Me Kill Me, With Or Without You, Moment Of Surrender, Bad / In The Garden / Walk On The Wild Side / 40.

My Musical Journey ended with Larry hugging me on his way to the stage of the last show in the U.S. on U2's 360 tour. I kept replaying it over and over in my head. Larry walking toward me, smiling, jumping down to me, putting his arms around me without saying a word, and hugging me. It seemed like it lasted forever, but after watching the videos, it was only a few seconds – but those were some magnificent few seconds! That was definitely my favorite moment of the tour and a perfect ending to my Musical Journey! I finally Found What I Was Looking For on the U2 360 Tour!

Post 360 Thoughts

I had always wanted to drive across the country, and I had always wanted to follow U2 on tour, not just shows here and there, but consecutively. That is exactly what I did on the last leg of the U2 360 Tour in 2011. I wasn't working and barely had enough money, but I packed up the car and Elvis, Cilla and I left our house for two and a half months to drive to every U2 show in the U.S. on the last leg of the 360 Tour. I skipped the Canada shows because I didn't want to take my dogs back and forth across the border several times.

On my musical journey, I visited great American sights, saw 16 magnificent U2 concerts and met many great people. Each 360 show had its special moments. My favorites were Anaheim2, Pittsburgh, St. Louis, Chicago and Seattle. I drove over 18,000 miles through 31 states – some states I drove through multiple times. My favorite cities were Palm Springs, Portland and Milwaukee. I really enjoyed my time out West. My favorite tourist sight I saw was by far Mount Rushmore. Along with the great U2 shows I went to and the great places I saw, I also made great friends and reconnected with old friends.

Before I planned to go on this epic two and a half month road trip to every U2 360 show in the U.S., I was kind of lost. I didn't know what I wanted to do with the rest of my life. I started a blog to document my trip and share it with others and then decided to write a book about all of my U2 travels. Through the U2 360 tour, I discovered I loved to write. Now I have a purpose, a direction. The U2 360 tour changed my life and helped me find what I've been looking for.

Besides giving my life a direction, the U2 360 Tour taught me many things. I learned there really is humidity in Southern California, to never drive around Chicago or Atlanta (especially on July 4th weekend), not to avoid an outdoor concert in Miami in the summer because you think it is going to be too hot because the shows in St. Louis, Baltimore and Nashville were much hotter, and U2 fans really are the greatest. But the most important lesson I learned is to always pursue your passion, even if you think it is impossible or impractical. If I had thought logically and practically, I would have skipped the second Anaheim show to make it an easier drive from California to Maryland to make it to the Baltimore show, but then I would have missed my favorite show of the tour. And if I had been thinking logically and practically, I would have never even gone on the two and a half month road trip to begin with because I couldn't really afford it, but then I would have missed out on the best summer of my life on the U2 360 Tour.

People say I am so lucky to have been to so many U2 shows and to have met the band etc. And I agree, I have been very fortunate, but it is not just dumb luck. I actually try really hard to get what I want. I have worked jobs that offer me the flexibility to travel and the availability to attend all these U2 shows. I don't have a family, which allows me the freedom to do what I want. I am different than most. My only goal has been to be happy, whatever that entails. I never had a goal to be married or to have a family. If that happened, it happened, but it wasn't a goal I was trying to achieve. My only goal has been to pursue my passion, whatever it takes. I have no regrets because I have always pursued my passions. It is better to regret something you have done, than something you haven't done.

www.ingramcontent.com/pod-product-compliance
Lightning Source LLC
LaVergne TN
LVHW051049080426
835508LV00019B/1782